# Kate and Ronnie Kray
# Murder, Madness and Marriage

*with Mandy Bruce*

BLAKE

Published by Blake Publishing Ltd,
98–100 Great North Road, London N2 0NL, England

First published in Great Britain in 1993

ISBN 1 85782 083 5



British Library Cataloguing-in-Publication Data:
A catalogue record for this book is available from the British Library.

Typeset by BMD Graphics, Hemel Hempstead

Printed by Cox and Wyman, Reading, Berkshire

1 3 5 7 9 10 8 6 4 2

For the kindest, most gentle man in the world – my Dad

I would also like to thank all the people who have helped me with this book, especially my brother-in-law Reggie Kray, Steph King, Frank and Noel, Mandy, John and Rosie, Ross and Sue D. Thank you for your support.

Love, Kate.

This book is written in my own words, but obviously it would never have been possible without the help and support of my husband, Ronnie

Kate is my wife and we will never be parted.
I have trusted her to help me tell the real story of the Krays today and she has.

RONNIE KRAY. BROADMOOR HOSPITAL,
BERKSHIRE, 1993

# CONTENTS

# *THEN*

# *Prologue: The Form*

*March, 1969.*
*The Old Bailey, London.*

'Ronald Kray. I am not going to waste words on you. The sentence is that of life imprisonment. In my view, society has earned a rest from your activities.'

'Reginald Kray. For the same reasons I have already indicated when dealing with your brother, Ronald, you will go to prison for life and I recommend that you also be detained for thirty years.'

For Mr Justice Melford Stevenson – known as 'the Hanging Judge' – it was the moment he had been waiting for, the climax of the longest murder trial in the history of Britain's Central Criminal Court, a high spot in his long legal career.

The Krays – identical twins – had stood in the dock facing their accusers for thirty-nine days. It took the jury six hours and fifty-four minutes to decide their guilt and, in sentencing them to life, with a recommendation of thirty years apiece, Judge Melford Stevenson was handing out the longest sentences for murder ever known at the Old Bailey.

The judge congratulated Detective Superintendent Leonard Read, who had led the investigation. For the policeman, known as 'Nipper' Read because he was like a little dog who never let go, it was a triumph. He and his team of nineteen officers – sixteen men and three women – had spent a year painstakingly collecting evidence and persuading reluctant witnesses to talk.

For gangsters Ronnie and Reggie Kray, who had virtually 'ruled' the East End for well over a decade, it was the end.

'We were both shattered, absolutely shocked by what we had heard,' Ronnie Kray later wrote in the twins' book, *Our Story*. 'We knew we would go down, knew we would get long sentences – but thirty years?'

And, much later, he told his wife, Kate: 'We both managed to put on a brave, defiant face to the world.

'But, once the screws had locked me up that night, I don't mind admitting I felt gutted.' Reggie, and the twins' elder brother, Charlie, who had been sentenced to ten years as an accessory to murder, felt the same despair.

Ronnie and Reggie were just thirty-four years old when they were put away for the murders of George Cornell and Jack 'The Hat' McVitie. But they'd come a long way from 178 Vallance Road, in Bethnal Green, later known by locals as 'Fort Vallance', where they grew up with brother Charlie, dad Charles senior and their much-loved mum, Violet.

As youngsters theirs was an East End where if you were going to make something of yourself in the world you had a choice: either to be a boxer or – a villain.

The twins, from an early age, loved boxing. They were ten when they went to a fairground which had temporarily pitched camp on a bombed-out site in Bethnal Green. They were immediately drawn to the 'Alf Stewart Boxing Booth' where members of the audience were challenged to fight the fairground boxers.

Any survivors who actually beat the fairground professionals were rewarded with a pound note.

The twins were thrilled and when, towards the end of the day, Alf Stewart invited members of the audience to jump into the ring to box for a few shillings, young Ronnie and Reggie volunteered straight away to fight each other. Ronnie ended up with a bleeding nose and Reggie with a black and blue, bruised face but they were paid 7s/6d and couldn't wait to get home and tell the family how they were now paid fighters.

The boys had a natural talent for boxing. Reggie became the schoolboy boxing champion of Hackney and then London Schools Champion. He was unbeaten as an amateur lightweight. Ron was good, too – he won Hackney schoolboy and London junior championships but sometimes he tended to let his temper get the better of him.

At twelve, the twins had their first write-up in a newspaper – the *Hackney Gazette*, who wrote about the young boxing Kray twins. Then the *Daily Mirror* came to take their picture and, by the time they were sixteen, family, neighbours and friends were quite used to reading about the boys in the press.

They were becoming somewhat notorious for their activities outside the ring, too. At sixteen they already had their own gang of local boys and they'd been barred from most of the cinemas and dance halls in East London.

Reggie admits that they used to sleep with knives and machetes under their beds in Vallance Road and they rarely left the house without carrying something they could use if they got into trouble.

'There were a lot of gang fights and we had to have weapons of some kind,' Reggie explained later.

Around the same time the boys acquired their first gun – from a local criminal – and first encountered the Old Bill. At the age of sixteen they were both charged with causing grievous bodily harm on three young men following a teenage gang fight where the chosen weapons were bicycle chains and coshes. Within months the twins were making their debut at the Old Bailey in Number One Court but, in part thanks to the efforts of their character witness, a vicar called the Reverend R. N. Hetherington who ran a youth club in Bethnal Green and remained a friend until his death, they were acquitted.

From then on the twins were involved in one scrap after another, but boxing remained their greatest interest. They turned professional as lightweights when they were seventeen. Reggie had seven professional fights and won every one. Ronnie fought six, winning four and losing two.

Out of the ring they were already beginning to be viewed as heavyweights, despite their young age. The Krays were beginning to get a reputation and, as far as Ronnie and Reggie were concerned, the future looked promising.

Until, that is, their lives were rudely interrupted by Her Majesty's Armed Forces. Ronald and Reginald Kray were called up to the Tower of London to join the Royal Fusiliers for National Service. By inclination and temperament neither of the twins was suited for the Army but, as Ronnie wrote later: 'We had a good chat about it and we decided that even though we were against the Army on principle, and even though we hated the thought of wearing a bloody uniform, we would give it a go as long as they would let us be PTIs, physical training instructors.'

So off they went in their best blue suits and informed the Army of their decision. The Army were not impressed and, in the person of a corporal – 'a bird brain who thought he was Winston Churchill', in Ronnie's opinion – the twins were informed that they'd have to do as they were told. So the twins made to leave, Ronnie smacking the corporal on the jaw on the way out as he tried to stop them. Within the hour they were back home in Vallance Road enjoying a cup of tea with their mum.

The twins did everything they could to get themselves thrown out of the Army and spent most of their Army career either absconding or in Army prisons paying the price for absconding. But Reggie later admitted to looking back on that time with nostalgia. 'When we were on the run we had some smashing times,' he said.

And, while serving time for desertion, they made some new friends – most notably Londoners Johnny Nash and Charlie Richardson, who would later head a rival gang south of the Thames.

Once they were discharged from the Army and back home in Vallance Road, the twins went into business with enthusiasm. They didn't specialise in any particular line of business – as long as it brought in the cash they were open to ideas – and they busied themselves with a variety of scams. They hired a crooked doctor and arranged exemption certificates from National Service for eighteen-year-olds. The boys' parents were only too happy to pay.

They sold watches which had been smuggled into the docks. These were duty-free, thus ensuring that a healthy profit was a cert. They stole lorry loads of goods: fruit, furniture, even aeroplane parts from an airbase.

Then they went into the club business which was to form the basis of their operations for many years to come. Their first big venture was a billiard hall called the Regal in Mile End. They were just twenty-one years old. The Regal was a rough place, frequently smashed up and terrorized by local thugs. The owner agreed to give Ronnie and Reggie the lease if they could keep the place under control and in one piece. Ron and Reg, who freely admitted to enjoying a good fight themselves, agreed. As soon as they took over the trouble stopped.

'It was very simple,' Reggie wrote later. 'The punters, the local tearaways, knew that if there was any trouble, if anything got broken, Ron and I would simply break their bones.'

It was the beginning of the Krays' protection racket. If they could protect their own business they could protect other people's...

The Krays were respected – and feared – and they had gathered around them their own crowd of 'employees', known as the Firm.

In 1957, Ronnie was sentenced at the Old Bailey to three years' imprisonment for grievous bodily harm on a man called Terry Martin after a fight outside a pub in Stepney. He also pleaded guilty to possessing a loaded revolver.

And it was while he was in prison that he was first certified as being insane.

'That's when my paranoia started,' Ron wrote later. 'I began feeling that people were plotting against me. If I saw two people chatting I was convinced they were planning how they were going to do me. So I just had to stop them, hurt them, make them see that what they were doing was wrong.'

Ronnie was sent to a mental hospital in Epsom. 'I was in an awful state. I thought the bloke in the opposite bed was a dog. I couldn't recognize anyone. I kept putting my hand through the glass in the windows. It was hell.'

Ronnie didn't stay in hospital for long. Brothers Reggie and Charlie hatched an ingenious escape plan. Reggie went to visit his twin and, once they were alone, they swopped clothes. Reggie walked in, but it was his identical twin Ronnie who walked out and, by the time the mistake was discovered, Ronnie was long gone. The hospital had no choice but to let Reggie go too.

Ron was on the run for 145 days before being recaptured by Scotland Yard detectives and taken back to prison. But he has suffered from the illness, chronic paranoid schizophrenia, ever since.

While Ron was away Reggie was approached by a friend who told him that a big, old house in Bow Road was an ideal building to convert into a nightclub. Reggie jumped at the chance and, after having the place redecorated, he opened what was to become the twins' most famous club of all, the Double R Club.

Years later he told his sister-in-law, Kate, that, looking back on his life, of the business deals he had handled alone, he was most proud of the setting up of the Double R. Upstairs, he installed a gym, which was opened by boxer Henry Cooper. Downstairs the club had luxurious, flocked wallpaper, a colourful bar and a small stage.

Reggie, and Ronnie when he came out, loved the Double R Club. Most nights they could be found at the bar socializing with their customers and sometimes their mum, Violet, who had a beautiful singing voice, would take to the stage and the microphone and treat the customers to a rendering of an Al Jolson song like 'Mammy' or 'Sonny Boy'.

Reggie was justifiably proud of the club. 'It was the first of its type in the East End of London,' he wrote later. 'A place where a man could take his mother, wife or fiancée for a drink in a respectable atmosphere.'

The Double R flourished and, in other ways too, business was booming. The twins became extremely adept at fraud and adapting business practices to their own advantage. Then there were the protection-rackets and a few second-hand-car businesses. They regularly hid, or sold on, stolen goods for other villains (for a percentage of the profits) and they ran a profitable line in money laundering.

After the success of the Double R there were more clubs, some of which they owned and several where they stayed in the background as silent partners. Esmerelda's Barn was a posh gambling club in Knightsbridge and, at one stage, they were also running an illegal gambling club situated immediately opposite Bow Police Station.

There was violence, too, but the twins regarded themselves as professionals. They lived by a code, the age-old code of villains in the East End. Recently Reggie published a book called *Villains We Have Known*, and he explained it like this:

> The people I have written about would not rape, hurt or harm, in any way, women or children or

> mug the elderly, they were mainly professional people of their chosen way of life.
>
> During the 1950s and 1960s these people were of a minority and had strong moral codes and ethics of their own standard and violence was kept within their own jungle. But today criminal boundaries have spilled out to national proportions, hence the lack of morals we see today, because many of the crimes committed cannot even be considered in a professional capacity.
>
> During the 1950s and 1960s it was like there was an official membership to what would be called an underworld and these people were known to each other and so were were the haunts used by them, and each one's actions were mainly known to the others, whereas today most of the criminal types are non-professional and belong to no particular group of people so their actions are not questioned by anyone of alliance.

Reggie's life was disrupted in 1959 when he was found guilty of demanding money with menaces and carted off for a year's stay in Wandsworth prison. But the years that followed were good ones for the Krays.

They had their problems, but their empire grew – and so did their name. Likewise their income. They still lived simply in the East End, at home with Violet in Vallance Road or in a variety of rented flats, but they were both snappy dressers in their smart, made-to-measure suits, they drove flash cars and often enjoyed the finest foods and drank the finest champagne.

And they were equally at home in an East End pub, enjoying a drink with their friends and business associates, and often they'd all end up going back to Vallance Road en masse to carry on with the party.

They were notoriously generous. If a neighbour was down on his luck they'd think nothing of helping out with a few hundred pounds. But, in return, they expected total loyalty.

They were becoming celebrities. People said that the police didn't lay down the law in London's East End, the Krays did. They looked after their own people and their own people looked after them. Cross one of the Kray 'Firm' and you paid the price.

The police were becoming increasingly irritated by these two young gangsters from Bethnal Green, not least because there was a glamour about them. Showbusiness stars flocked to their new club, the Kentucky, in Stepney, a plush place with deep red carpets, mirrors and gold 'antique' furniture. Stars like Diana Dors, Barbara Windsor, Shirley Bassey, Judy Garland, Sophie Tucker and Winifred Atwell were all photographed enjoying a drink with the Krays in their clubs.

Among their friends Ronnie and Reggie counted the most famous boxers of the time, politicians, aristocracy. All were attracted to the Krays like bees to a honeypot. It made them feel that they were living dangerously.

The twins enjoyed their success but, personally, life was not so simple. Ronnie's illness worried Reggie and the rest of the family, and his emotional life was never very stable. As everyone knew, Ron was a bisexual who had had a string of affairs with pretty young men.

Reggie always had a eye for the girls until he met and fell head over heels in love with a beautiful local girl called Frances Shea. Her parents didn't approve of the match but, nevertheless, Reggie and Frances married on 19 April 1965 and in Bethnal Green it was the wedding of the year.

Two years later Frances committed suicide and Reggie was devastated. Much later he wrote: 'Part of me died when Frances died and I stopped caring about things. The rest of me died when my mother passed away.'

But in 'business' it appeared the twins couldn't fail. As the 1960s drew to a swinging close it seemed that nothing and no one could stop the Krays. There were calls for the police to clamp down on London's criminal gangs but the twins seemed to be untouchable. They went from strength to strength. Everyone, including the American Mafia, wanted to do business with the Krays and, as a result, Ron flew to New York to meet with the Mafia bosses there and Ronnie and Reggie were soon repaying their hospitality in London.

Business was going well, very well. The twins bought more clubs, including the Cambridge Rooms on the Kingston by-pass which opened with a grand party attended by, among others, the great Sonny Liston, then heavyweight champion of the world.

The twins were enjoying the good life – they bought a big house in the country and even a racehorse for their mum called Solway Cross. It turned out to be a no-hoper and they quickly donated it to be given away at a charity raffle. They travelled – to Germany, Italy, France, Ibiza, Casablanca, Tangier (from where they were extradited),

Turkey (Ron still has fond and vivid memories of his two favourite visits – to a mosque and a brothel) and Jersey (where he loved the beaches and the countryside).

They were making money hand over fist. But there were problems. The twins were tempted into a business deal involving a company with plans to build houses and factories in Nigeria. Ronnie and Reggie were enthusiastic but they were looking for other backers.

Someone suggested that Lord Boothby, once a Tory MP for Aberdeenshire and a famous political figure, might be interested in investing in the project. Ronnie Kray duly met him. The resulting publicity was, as far as the twins were concerned, just what they didn't need.

There were stories about an alleged homosexual affair between a top London gangster and a peer of the realm, and allegations of blackmail. The newspapers began a campaign urging the Home Secretary to crack down on the Krays and other London gangs. Lord Boothby later won an apology and £40,000 damages from IPC, the publishers of the *Sunday Mirror*, and Ronnie has always denied that he ever had a homosexual relationship with Lord Boothby.

'It was strictly a business arrangement,' Ronnie wrote later, 'which became a friendship – a friendship based on the fact that we had both been so badly smeared by the national press.'

And he went on: 'The publicity the Krays received at that time undoubtedly helped us towards our downfall. Suddenly we were major celebrities, and suddenly, also, we were right at the top of the Metropolitan Police hit list.'

Ronnie was right. Not long afterwards Reggie was sentenced to six months, which he spent in Wandsworth prison, for involvement in a protection racket which went wrong. Then Ronnie was accused of housebreaking, but the case was dismissed. They were both charged with loitering with intent – again the case was dismissed.

In many ways, 1966 was the year that the twins could look back on as the beginning of the end. The scene was being set for the drama that was to be played out in the Central Criminal Court three years later.

The Krays became involved in a feud with the Richardsons, a south London gang led by Charlie Richardson, whom they knew from their Army days, and his brother, Eddie. There was another gang fight, one of many, this time in a club called Mr Smith's in Catford and, although the twins weren't there at the time, one of the Firm, a young man called Richard Hart, was shot. Charlie and Eddie Richardson, and another member of their gang, Frankie Fraser, were arrested for their part in what happened, but one man escaped arrest.

He was George Cornell, someone the twins believed was intent on stirring trouble for them. Ronnie, particularly, disliked him intensely.

The legendary story goes that at a meeting between the Richardsons and the Krays, to discuss the American Mafia connection, George Cornell said of Ronnie: 'Take no notice of Kray. He's just a big fat poof.'

Ronnie, who hated any reference to his sexuality, could not forget the remark. And Richard Hart's death had to avenged.

On 9 March 1966 – almost three years to the day before

being sentenced to life at the Old Bailey – Ronnie Kray heard that Cornell was drinking in a pub called The Blind Beggar in Whitechapel Road in London's Stepney. As Reggie said later, Ronnie always hated that pub – he said it was a dump. Ronnie says that perhaps he had a premonition about what was to happen in the place.

Ronnie told Reggie that it was about time they dealt with Cornell. 'I'm going to do the bastard.'

Ron carried a Luger gun in the right-hand pocket of his overcoat. His driver took him to the Blind Beggar, he walked in and found Cornell in the near-empty pub drinking with two of his associates. Ron took the gun out of his pocket, aimed at Cornell's head and fired. Cornell died before he hit the carpet.

Cornell's drinking partners dived for the floor, as did the two or three other customers who'd been sitting quietly nursing their pints. The barmaid screamed. The record on the jukebox jammed and started to blast out the line of the song it was playing again and again: 'The sun ain't gonna shine any more, the sun ain't gonna shine any more . . .'

Ron returned to Reggie, who was drinking in another pub, and told him what he'd done. They immediately made their way to yet another pub where Ronnie scrubbed his hands to remove any powder marks and changed into a new, clean set of clothes which members of the Firm had picked up from his flat.

Another friend, Charlie Clark, a burglar known as the Cat Man, disposed of the gun.

Ronnie and Reggie had a few drinks and sandwiches and turned on the 'Nine o'Clock News' to hear that there had been a fatal shooting in the East End.

Later, back home, the police arrived and took both of them into custody for questioning. They declared their innocence and the eyewitnesses, who had been in the Blind Beggar, could not pick them out on an identity parade. The twins were released.

The police could prove nothing. No one was talking. But they knew – as everyone who knew anything about anything in the East End knew – that Ronnie Kray had killed George Cornell. Now he had really lived up to his nickname of the 'Colonel', given to him by the Firm because of the precise way in which he organized 'business' and because he loved battles.

The fact that one of the twins had killed a man, 'done' one of Krays' enemies, only did more to enhance their reputation and inspire more loyalty, respect – and fear.

And the Cornell episode did nothing to dampen the twins' enthusiasm for their business activities. Fully aware that the police were now taking an almost obsessive interest in them, they laid low and took a holiday in Tangier for a few weeks. But, once home again, they fell easily back into their old routine.

Ironically, although 1966 was the year of the beginning of the end for Ronnie and Reggie, it was also the year of what has since been described as their greatest coup: the springing of a villain called Frank Mitchell – known as the 'Mad Axeman' – from Dartmoor prison.

They planned the escape with care. Reggie even did a recce and made a trip to Dartmoor. He contacted a friend, former world boxing champion Ted Lewis, and asked him to write to the prison's Governor offering to give a talk to the cons about his boxing career and show some films of his fights.

Ted mentioned that he would be accompanied by three friends. Of course Ted had no idea why his friends wanted to visit Dartmoor. Unbeknown to the authorities one of them was Reggie who, just for fun, also brought along two of his friends, ex-cons with long lists of convictions. An enjoyable day out was had by all – especially as the Governor treated Ted and his group to a splendid meal after the show and urged them all to 'Call again.' With a straight face, Reggie assured him they'd be delighted.

Shortly afterwards Frank Mitchell was with an outside working party when he quietly slipped away from the other prisoners. At a pre-arranged point, he met two members of the Firm, who bundled him into a car. He was back in London before he had even been missed.

For a while the Krays hid him in a London flat then, one night, he was due to move to another safe house in the country. He left in a van with members of the Firm – and was never seen again.

By now stories about the Krays were rife in London, both in the West and East End – and in Scotland Yard.

There was the famous tale about George Dixon, a villain whom Ronnie had barred from the twins' Regency Club because of his heavy drinking.

Dixon ignored the ban and walked into the club where he found Ronnie, a far from welcoming host, sitting at the bar. Ronnie took a revolver, held it to Dixon's head and pulled the trigger. Nothing happened. The gun had jammed.

Dixon ran for his life – and Ronnie later gave him the

bullet which should have killed him as a souvenir. Forever afterwards Dixon wore it on a chain around his neck as a good-luck charm.

This notoriety earned Ronnie and Reggie respect from fellow villains but, increasingly, it also meant more and more attention from the police. The twins, who had always had good police contacts, were warned that two officers – Fred Gerrard and someone called Nipper Read – were making more than the usual inquiries about them and that they were compiling a comprehensive dossier on the Krays and their activities. The word was that they'd been told to 'get the Krays' however long it took.

After a while, Ronnie was convinced that, if they were ever going to be put away for a long time, it would be Nipper Read who turned the key in the lock, But, to the outside world, the twins appeared unruffled.

Both Ronnie and Reggie had always been animal lovers –Reggie's favourite pet was a pekinese dog he called Mitzi and Ron was always buying pedigree dogs. He also bought a donkey which he used to bring into the Kentucky Club. Now the Kray brothers bought themselves two snakes as pets, which they fed with live mice and called Nipper and Gerrard.

They used to laugh when the snakes kept escaping from their tank and, knowing their phone was being tapped, enjoyed telling any members of the Firm who rang: 'I'm just going to feed Gerrard and Nipper.'

But Read and Gerrard's inquiries turned out to be no laughing matter. The Krays' luck was running out.

By 1967 the twins' anger was concentrated on a man who had been a member of their own Firm, a man called Jack 'The Hat' McVitie. McVitie was becoming increasingly arrogant. On one occasion he was drunk and had gone into the Regency Club brandishing a sawn-off shotgun and shouting threats at members of the Firm and, more foolishly, at Ronnie and Reggie themselves. They weren't there but they received a full report of what happened.

McVitie was a liability. He had taken one liberty too many. Reggie and Ronnie agreed that he had to go. Reggie went looking for McVitie without success. Finally, one October night, the twins made sure that an inebriated McVitie attended a party in a flat in Stoke Newington.

When he arrived Reggie drew out a .32 automatic, pointed it at McVitie's head and pulled the trigger. Nothing happened. It was the Dixon story all over again but for McVitie there was no reprieve. Desperate, McVitie tried to get away. The door was blocked by members of the Firm so he dived through the window. Broken glass and wood from the window frame scattered over the room but McVitie's body was stuck.

Two of the Firm pulled him back by the legs and then held him while Reggie stabbed him in the chest, neck and face until he was dead.

There was a lot of blood. Members of the Firm cleaned the flat while others wrapped up the body in a bedspread and drove off to dispose of it. Reggie and Ronnie made their escape to a friend's flat to clean up and then left for a friend's house in the country where they stayed for a week or so.

Over the following months the police were busy. Slowly, patiently, they persuaded witnesses to talk.

On 8 May 1968 the twins were out on the town having a few drinks with their friends. They stopped off at the Astor Club in Berkeley Square and they noticed one or two plain-clothes detectives mingling with the customers, but thought nothing of it. By now they were quite accustomed to being watched.

But at six the following morning, in Ron's flat at Cedra Court in Bunhill Road, Walthamstow, while the twins were asleep, Nipper Read and his team, all carrying .45 calibre Webleys, kicked down the front door.

The twins were arrested.

Ronnie and Reggie were charged with the murders of Cornell, McVitie and, later, Frank Mitchell (a charge of which they were acquitted). And there was a long list of other charges, several involving fraud and demanding money with menaces.

Another bizarre accusation was that they had hired a hitman to kill one of their enemies while he was actually in the Old Bailey. The weapon was supposedly going to be an attaché case fitted with a hypodermic syringe full of poison which would be activated when the case was swung against the victim's body. That charge was later dropped.

Ron was also charged with causing grievous bodily harm to a man in one of his clubs. The prosecution alleged that, because the man had annoyed him, Ron had invited him into the club, paid the man's taxi fare and then put a red-hot poker on his cheeks and shoulders.

The Firm had been rounded up and, along with the Krays' elder brother Charlie, were charged with a variety of offences. Nipper Read had always maintained that the only way he would nail the Krays was if he could get other criminals to testify against them.

As John Pearson wrote in his biography of the Krays – *The Profession of Violence*:

> They [the police] had the few weeks before the preliminary hearings to clinch their case and persuade their major witnesses to talk. They knew exactly who they were, but had to be able to assure them that this time the twins were finished. Otherwise, as one old cockney put it, 'If people talk to the police and the twins get off again, they'll have to send the plague carts into Bethnal Green and shout, "Bring out your dead!"'

But, to the everlasting disgust of Ronnie and Reggie, many of the Firm turned 'grass' and talked.

The reign of the Krays was over.

Twenty-five years on the twins are still locked up. At first, Ronnie was sent to Durham jail and Reggie to Parkhurst. After seventeen years as a Category A high-profile prisoner, Reggie was marked down to Category A, and then B, and, after stays in Gartree and Lewes prisons, he's now in Blundestone, Suffolk.

After a series of fights in prison, Ronnie was again certified as insane and sent to Broadmoor Hospital, where he is still a high-profile prisoner, guarded night and day.

When they appeared together in the dock they pleaded not guilty to all charges – but since being convicted they have never pleaded innocence. Yet both say they have, by now, paid their debt to society.

The year of the Krays' trial, 1969, was the year man first walked on the moon – although to the young, at least, Carnaby Street was still the centre of the universe. The Rolling Stones played a free concert in Hyde Park before half a million people in memory of Brian Jones, who had recently died. The ten-shilling note was replaced by the 50p coin and a plane called Concorde had just taken to the sky. President Nixon visited Britain, President De Gaulle resigned and a fresh-faced, twenty-one-year-old Charles was invested as Prince of Wales at Caernarvon Castle.

On 24 October 1993, the twins celebrate their sixtieth birthdays.

During their trial 'tickets' for the public gallery at the Old Bailey were changing hands for five pounds – a lot of money in those days. The Krays were big box-office.

Twenty-five years after they were taken into custody they remain big box-office. In March 1993, over 300 people paid twenty pounds a head to attend a get-together of Kray 'fans' in a London club. It was so successful that two more parties were planned for later the same year.

Twenty-five years on, they still hold a fascination for thousands of people. There have been numerous books written about them, their faces appear on t-shirts, and the recent film, *The Krays*, starring the Kemp brothers of Spandau Ballet, was a smash hit.

They've become a modern legend and the myths that surround them are legion. What they did – or what they didn't do – is still a matter of debate.

Twenty-five years on, for many people, the name Kray still inspires loyalty, respect – and fear.

And, for one woman, who was a child when the Krays were kings, it has meant love and marriage. This year Kate and Ronnie Kray celebrate their fourth wedding anniversary. A funny kind of love – a funny kind of liberty.

This is her story, hers and Ronnie's – and the story of the Krays, twenty-five years on...

*M.B.*
July, 1993

# *NOW*

## CHAPTER ONE

# *Tying the Knot*

*Monday, 6 November 1989.*
*Broadmoor Hospital for the Criminally Insane.*

'Do you Kathleen Anne take Ronald for your lawful wedded husband? Do you promise to love, honour and keep him as long as you both shall live?'

'I do-Ron-Ron, I do!'

Well, at least it broke the ice. Until then the room had been dead quiet and the atmosphere a bit chilly – I don't think our guests felt very comfortable with all those screws standing around watching them. But now I turned around and grinned at the eight men sitting solemnly, all suit-to-boot, in rows behind us and they started laughing.

Ron smiled and gave me a big kiss.

'Nice one, Ron!' said his mates. Ron laughed.

We signed the marriage certificate and that was that. I was officially Mrs Ronnie Kray. Kate Kray. It has a nice ring to it. It felt right – it still does.

The courtship had been odd, I suppose, by normal standards – no sex for a start, no time alone together even – and the wedding was bizarre to say the least.

From the very start it was a crazy day. I'd spent the night before at Harry's place. He's my best friend – and my ex-husband – and he lives in a little country cottage down the road from me in Headcorn, not far from Maidstone. Like all brides the first thing I did was open the curtains and take a look at the weather. A freezing, grey winter's day. But at least it wasn't raining.

I put the kettle on and Harry went off to take the dog for his early-morning walk. He's a wire-haired fox terrier and I got him in Wales so we call him Taffy. Ron wanted me to call him 'The 'Colonel', since that's what everyone calls him and, true, the dog's bloody mad and fearless at times, but I wasn't having that! Too soppy!

Funnily enough, I wasn't nervous that morning. I'd slept all right and I felt quite calm. But it was weird: I turned on Radio One and suddenly there was this bloke saying: 'Ronnie Kray, the notorious gangster, is getting married today in Broadmoor. His bride is Kate Howard...'

That's me, I thought, that's me they're talking about. But it didn't sound like me at all. It was as if I was listening to news of someone else – not me and Ron. But Ron always says that famous people are only famous until you meet them and get to know them, and that then they are as normal as you and me.

Within minutes Harry was back with Taffy. 'Christ,' he said. 'There's dozens of photographers out there.'

I looked out of the window, but I couldn't see a soul.

'They're all parked up the road,' said Harry.

The next moment the phone rang. It was one of the reporters outside. He wanted a photo of me. I said I was going to the hairdresser's.

'Great,' he said, 'we'll take photos of you at the hairdresser's.'

'Leave it out,' I said. Was he mad? There's not a woman alive who'd have her picture taken at the hairdresser's, especially on her wedding day.

So they took my photo outside the cottage and off I

went to have my hair done, pulled up in a French roll and off my face. Ron wanted me to wear my hair down around my shoulders; he likes women to wear their hair long. I said no, he wasn't going to have his own way with everything.

After I'd had my hair done, Harry and I got into our gold Rolls-Royce to drive up to the Hilton Hotel in Bracknell just a few miles from Broadmoor. The photographers went snap, snap but I didn't feel a thing. I didn't feel nervous. I didn't feel apprehensive or worried or even particularly excited. It was a strange feeling; I was numb, almost in a dreamworld, as if this was all happening to somebody else and I was just sitting back there in the car, watching.

Everyone said the Roller was a present from Ron. It wasn't; I should be so lucky! At the time, Harry and I were running a chauffeur business and the car was the one we used to take people to parties and weddings – the only car, in fact.

We hadn't had it very long and I was very fond of it. The day I bought it, I went to see Ron and told him I was going up to London on the train to collect it and that I was going to pay in cash.

'Be careful, Kate,' Ron warned me. 'Don't carry the cash in a bag – you could easily get mugged. Put the money in pockets all over your body. It's harder to nick.'

So that's what I did. You should have seen the salesman's face when I produced fivers and tenners out of all the pockets of my jeans and jacket!

Preparing for any wedding is hectic, but ours was more complicated than most – well, if you're marrying someone like Ron, who's still reckoned to be a dangerous criminal and who's still inside, I suppose you have to expect a few snags. And we arranged the whole thing in under four weeks! Ron had been proposing off and on for a year and as soon as I finally said yes he said: 'Right, let's do it as soon as possible.'

First, we'd had to get permission from the Governor at Broadmoor and I'd been interviewed by Ron's doctors, who explained his illness to me. Did I know this man? Did I know what I was doing? Was I really convinced it was the right thing? I didn't feel nervous about seeing them because I had all the answers. I didn't have to lie. I was doing the right thing. I didn't doubt it, and I knew that Ron felt the same way, although he did keep saying I might be taking on more than I'd bargained for. But I thought that was just Ron being Ron – concerned for me.

Because Ron had been married before – and me too, twice – the Broadmoor chaplain refused to marry us in the hospital chapel. That was a shame. You may find it hard to believe but, quietly, Ron has a deep faith in God and he's found this belief increasingly comforting after so many years inside. He says now: 'I don't have to answer to anybody. I'm my own man. I've only got one judge and that's the Lord God Almighty. He can judge me. No one else.' And he's quite philosophical about getting out. As far as Ron's concerned God will decide when – and if.

The vicar said he'd be happy to bless the ceremony in the chapel afterwards, but first I had to arrange for the local registrar from Bracknell to come in and perform the legal marriage ceremony. She turned out to be a lovely lady; she said she'd organize the banns, and almost in the same breath swore she wouldn't breathe a word of our plans to anyone.

That was a relief, and I honestly thought we might manage to keep the whole thing a secret. That was just me being naïve. The registrar really needn't have worried. One of the nurses at Broadmoor tipped off the press as soon as he heard. Ron said it was to be expected. Maybe it made the bloke a few bob, and if it did, good luck to him.

For three weeks I was running around like a nutter getting everything ready. Like most men, Ron didn't want to know much about the arrangements once I'd said yes: 'That's your business,' he said. 'You sort it.'

He told me to look for a wedding ring and I saw just what I was looking for by chance up in town in a jeweller's window. I didn't want an ordinary wedding band. I wanted something different and special and there it was: a band of gold studded with diamonds and rubies. Perfect. But it was also a perfectly naughty price: £750. I put a small deposit on it and went and told Ron.

'Buy it,' he said, and when he saw it he was very pleased. He said it was the most beautiful wedding ring he'd ever seen. I wanted to wear it there and then, but Ron wouldn't hear of it. He took it to look after and I had to wait for my wedding day for it to be slipped on my finger.

But apart from the ring – and me – all Ron was interested in was the guest list.

I'd told very few people about the wedding. Reggie knew, of course, and Harry. 'I knew you'd marry one of them,' he said. Then I drove down to Kent, where Mum and Dad were living in a trailer, to tell them.

Dad was mowing their little lawn when I arrived and there was no point in beating around the bush, so I came straight out with it. They knew I'd been seeing Ron, but the fact that we'd get married probably never crossed their minds.

'By the way, Dad, I'm marrying Ronnie Kray...'

He stopped mowing. Then he looked at me, smiled, and raised his eyes to the sky as if to say: 'Oh my God, what's she doing now?' Then he went on mowing! He's the most precious man in the world to me, but never much of a one for words!

Mum seemed pleased. 'If that's what you want, then do it,' she said.

I took them both down to Broadmoor to see Ron and I could tell that Dad was all right but that Mum was really nervous. The first time you go to Broadmoor it gets you like that. And she didn't know what to expect from Ron. I think she thought he'd be big and brash, but he's not like that at all. He gave her a kiss and sat her down next to him and soon they were chatting away – at least Mum was chatting away, saying the usual embarrassing things that mums do about what a cow I was, etc!

Dad really liked him, and Ron liked them both. He's not one for small talk but he was friendly and my mum adored him. Ron has a way with women; he's a right old charmer when he wants to be. The Smiling Viper, I call him when I'm not in too nice a mood, especially when I hear another couple of women have been down to fawn over him. There's so many who go down and see him – Lady This and Lady That, all sorts – and they all come out the same, saying: 'Oooh, isn't he lovely!'

Ron didn't ask Mum and Dad for permission to marry me. He didn't have to. In fact, we hardly mentioned the wedding at all. But I was glad that they got on so well and they still do. Every time Mum goes on holiday she buys him a little something and every now and then Ron sends her flowers without even telling me.

Dad, for some reason, always calls Ron 'Jack the Hat'. Every time he sees me he goes, 'Er, how's Jack the Hat then?' and he starts laughing. I told Ron and he thought it was really funny.

But there was no way Mum and Dad could come to the wedding ceremony. Broadmoor said we could have just eight guests at the hospital and, Ron being Ron, there were close friends he had to have there – people who would have been very offended if they hadn't been invited. And Broadmoor also said that they had to be people who had visited Ron often over the years, so that cut Mum and Dad out anyway.

When I saw Ron he had the list: seven men and one woman to support me! I chose a friend of mine called Sharon. She's a nice girl, and she was also the only girlfriend of mine who had ever visited Ron inside, and so she was acceptable to Broadmoor.

Then there was Ron's brother Charlie, of course, and Joey Pyle – Mr Big the newspapers call him – who's been a good friend of Ron and Reggie's for a long time. Not so long ago he was branded Britain's number-one criminal by one newspaper, and he's now serving fourteen years for smuggling drugs worth half a million pounds.

I don't know about all that, but I've always liked Joey.

He was there the first time I met Ron at Broadmoor and he's always been very friendly to me. He's a big and stocky man, always very smartly dressed. I've always thought he looks a bit like Terry Venables. In fact, when I was with a girlfriend in a restaurant once, and the waiter told us a bloke wanted to send us over a drink, I thought it was Joey. It wasn't – it was Terry Venables!

Next there was Alec Steen, a London boxing promoter. Alec is a real dude and looks more like a gangster than a gangster does! He always wears a long, white mac over his suit and a pair of shades. He wears those dark glasses whatever the weather, day or night, all the time – weddings included!

And there was Wilf Pine, another old friend of Ron's. Wilf is about fifty now, with grey hair and a grey beard. He is another smartly-dressed man. To look at him you wouldn't believe his age, and he has two young babies with his lovely wife, Roz. He's a businessman working in the film and music industry and he used to be the manager of the band Black Sabbath.

Then there was Johnny Nash, one of the Nash brothers, who are both businessmen from east London. Ron wanted to invite him. He struck me as a very quiet man and I liked him when I met him at the wedding, although I haven't seen him from that day to this.

Another guest was Paul Lake, a very talented young artist who'd painted Eric Clapton and was doing a picture of the twins at the time. He's a good-looking chap and really nice too, but I don't think his painting of Ron and Reg was one of his greatest successes. It's one of the most horrible paintings I've ever seen. Reggie looks like a Toby jug and Ron looks like he's just bitten someone's head off!

There was one other man whose name I can't remember, who was doing a bit of business with Ron at the time, and finally Ron's best man, another patient at Broadmoor called Charlie Smith. Charlie is Ron's best friend in Broadmoor, and like so many people there, his story is a tragic one. He's in his mid-thirties now but he's been away since he was seventeen.

Ron is very anti-drugs; he always has been and meeting Charlie has only made him more so. Almost any young teenager could find himself in young Charlie's position if he gets involved in drugs. Charlie started on drugs when he was very young and one day while he was high he stabbed a man. Once he came down and realized what he had done, he gave himself up to the police and, of course, was put in prison. But Charlie wasn't well. No one seemed to realize that he needed help and he didn't get any. He then went completely mad, and strangled his cellmate, so they put him in Broadmoor. He's been there now for nearly fifteen years with no release date.

All our wedding guests had to be checked out by the Home Office, I'm not entirely sure why. I shouldn't think the SAS could get anyone out of Broadmoor and you'd have to be some kind of mega-magician to smuggle anything in. But there was one other guest Ron wanted to invite who the Home Office turned down flat. This was Charlie Richardson, a London gangster Ron had known from the old days. God knows why they wouldn't let Charlie come. Ron was a bit upset about it. Ron and Reggie and Charlie Richardson go back a long way. They all met in Shepton Mallet prison, where the twins were doing nine months after deserting from the Army. That was in 1953 – three years before I was born!

I suppose some people might be surprised that Ron wanted Charlie at our wedding at all. After all, the Kray and Richardson gangs had been at each other's throats back in the old days, sometimes literally. And, of course, George Cornell, who Ron shot, was a member of the Richardson team.

But that was all a very long time ago and Ron and Charlie are good friends now. Charlie visits him in Broadmoor and I know Ron looks forward to those days. Only recently Ron gave Charlie a beautiful 1950s solid silver cigarette case.

The one other guest – probably the most important one – who was supposed to come but didn't was Reggie. Broadmoor had even said that he could stay overnight in one of the rooms – they don't call them cells – and be driven back in the morning.

But Ron and Reg had a right old tear-up – which I'll explain later – just before the wedding, and Reg said he wasn't going to come. So Ron said: 'Don't bloody come, then.' Then Reg said he would and then he said he wouldn't and then he said he would. In the end the nick said, 'Sod it, too much mucking about, you're not going,' and that was that.

Ron and I really wanted the wedding to be a day to remember, something special, so, since only eight people could come to the proper service, we decided to throw a big party at the Bracknell Hilton for Ron's closest friends on the outside.

It was a frantic time. I was organizing both wedding parties and visiting Ron every other day. All he could talk about was the list. That's one job he had to do himself; I couldn't do it because I didn't know the people and anyway he thought it would be a liberty if someone somewhere along the line didn't get invited.

'Put this one on, he's gotta come, he's not coming but he can come...' What with all the other arrangements, it nearly did my head in! Ron wrote to invite some of them and I phoned others. Suddenly all kinds of people came out of the woodwork and wanted to come to show their respect for Ron. But we couldn't have everyone Ron knew – we'd never find a place big enough for a start – so we had to keep it to Ron's closest friends. Even so, by the time we'd finished, the list had 200 names on it!

None of my friends – apart from Harry and Sharon – were on the list and I didn't invite any of my family, either. That probably seems strange but I knew I would have enough on my plate without having to keep the family entertained and I could could hardly introduce them to people I didn't know myself. And then there'd be my mum, bless her, trying to make conversation, saying things like 'Did you meet Ron in prison?' and my dad saying 'I'm glad she's married Jack the Hat' and laughing. Ron laughs at that, too, but I don't know if all his friends would have seen the joke!

Broadmoor allowed me to see the room where we were going to have the ceremony and my heart sank. It was what they call the Tribunal Room, where the patients go to hear if they've got parole, and it's a grim, stark room painted in that cream and green they seem to save for prisons and old hospitals. There were bars at the windows and awful orange-and-brown diamond patterned curtains which must have been hanging there since the 1960s. There was a little bookcase full of little silver trophies and that was it. It was horrible.

I pulled the ugly curtains and I didn't know which was worse: the curtains or the bars at the windows. In the end I decided the curtains were worse, so we kept them drawn back.

'Right,' I said to the catering manager, 'I want a hundred pink-and-white balloons with trailing ribbons falling from the ceiling.' He was really great. After I'd seen the room, we went and saw Ron who, being a typical man, wasn't that interested.

'I don't know about all this stuff. You sort it.'

So me and the catering manager did just that. He said they'd put up one table for the registrar and another big one for the food and drinks, both covered with nice white cloths. If I arranged for the florist to come in, they could garland them with fresh flowers and greenery. And they'd lend us Broadmoor's best china and silver cutlery.

'As for the food, as long as you pay for it you can have whatever you like,' he said. Can't say fairer than that. So I ordered lobster and caviar, more seafood and prawns, turkey for people who didn't like fish and Caesars salads. To drink there would be champagne and soft drinks, and he offered to make us a two-tier pink-and-white wedding cake in the shape of a heart.

It was all going to cost quite a bit – £400 for the do at Broadmoor – although Charlie, as best man, was treating us to most of that as a wedding present. But the party at the Hilton was going to set us back £700. Still, we thought, it was worth it. We'd also decided to dress for the occasion – Ron's suit cost £800, which I thought made my £600 dress seem quite a bargain!

The photographs were a problem. David Bailey had agreed to do the photos for us. He's an old friend, and he actually took the photographs at Reggie's wedding years ago when he married his much-loved Frances.

But then a story appeared in the papers, saying that we were going to sell the photos for bundles of money, and Broadmoor weren't having that. So we had to cancel Bailey and Broadmoor got us Ron Francis, the photographer who goes up there every year to take up-to-date pictures of the prisoners in case any of them do a bunk. They trusted him.

By the time I checked into the Hilton I still had the feeling that none of this was happening to me. But I was beginning to feel that first tingle of excitement, all mixed up with nerves. Harry was in one room, with me in another and Sharon just down the hall. I was really glad she was there, grateful for some female company.

I was having a bath, and Sharon stood looking out of the bedroom window, when she called me over: 'Kate, come here, take a look!'

Outside were dozens of photographers, lined up on the grassy banks like some kind of army waiting to fight. Suddenly I felt sick, and for the first time really nervous.

Sharon laced me into my dress. I'd had it made for me by a girl called Aneska, and it was a boned basque top with a double skirt, all in peach silk and trimmed with cream silk roses. It was gorgeous and I had cream silk shoes decorated with peach roses to match. My bouquet was keeping fresh in the hotel sink – peachy pink roses and white freesias – and I wore silk roses in my hair.

'Come on,' said Harry, who was going to chaffeur me to Broadmoor in the Rolls. 'Let's go.'

The hotel were great. They let us slip out of the back delivery door and the hotel manager and his security men crowded round me so the press couldn't see my dress. Then we drove off up the driveway and it was madness. There were photographers flashing their cameras like mad and photographers coming out of the bushes and photographers hurling themselves at the bonnet of the car.

I was already too nervous to be nervous, but Harry said, 'What the fuck's going on?' He was terrified he'd run one of them over. I just sat there in a state of shock.

There were more waiting for us outside Broadmoor and Harry dodged them like traffic cones. But the Broadmoor screws made them clear a way for us and we swept through the big gates. There are two lots of gates and you have to stop between them to have your identity checked. One of the screws came over. Our guests, it seemed, had all arrived. He was laughing. 'It's just like a Mafia convention in there, Kate,' he said. I burst out laughing.

Sharon and I signed in and Harry drove the Rolls into the courtyard. He couldn't leave the car unattended – although who would nick it I can't imagine – so he was staying with it, and Sharon and I went up to the Tribunal Room. There were the men, all in their big-shouldered suits and Alec in his white mac and the dark glasses. But Ron hadn't been brought up yet, so they took Sharon and me into another room. It wouldn't do for the bride to be there before the bridegroom.

Then we were called in. Ron was standing in front of the white table. He looked me up and down, and when he saw the roses on my shoes he started laughing. 'You look like Little Bo Beep with those bleeding things on the end of your feet!' he said.

The first thing I noticed was his suit. I'd bought him two made-to-measure in Cashmere: one in Prince of Wales check, the other a lovely navy-blue. Wear the navy-blue, I'd said to him. So, of course, he was wearing the Prince of Wales check!

There were loads of screws standing round the room, more than two for each guest. What were they expecting – a riot? But they'd probably never seen such a group before – at least such a group who were going to be allowed to walk out in a hour or so! And it was really quiet. The men didn't like it with all those screws there. No one knew what to say. It was terrible, really.

Then the registrar asked Ron and me some details. Father's occupation? 'Carpenter,' I said. Ron thought for a moment. 'Wardrobe dealer,' he said. I looked at him. 'Wardrobe dealer?' I mouthed silently and started laughing. 'Well, it's true,' he whispered and it was. Years ago, that's what they used to call men who went totting from house to house.

Occupation? 'Proprietress of a chaffeur Rolls-Royce service,' I wrote. The registrar looked at Ron and he smiled and, with a definite twinkle in his eyes, he looked straight into hers. 'Err,' she said and smiled back, 'I think we'll leave that blank.'

And then we had the ceremony. For weeks Ron had been winding me up, saying that when it came to it he'd throw himself on the floor and pretend to have a fit. 'That will give them something to talk about,' he said. 'Don't you dare!' I said.

But when they asked him if he took Kathleen Anne as his lawful wife he just looked at me and said, 'Yeah.' And he slipped the ruby-and-diamond ring on my finger.

Immediately afterwards the vicar came and went with us to the chapel for the blessing. It's a beautiful little church with lovely stained-glass windows. We knelt down before the altar and repeated our vows again and said a couple of prayers together. It was really very nice, very special. But they would only allow two people – Charlie, the best man, and Ron's friend, Wilf – to go with us, and Ron was well annoyed about that. I mean, what harm could it have done for the others to come too?

We went back to the Tribunal Room and our little reception began. It wasn't long before Ron left me to talk in a huddle with his friends. 'Kate,' he said, 'I don't get much chance to talk to my friends – not all together.' And off he went. I understood. Ron is Ron and business is business and business comes first even if you have just got married!

So I was left talking to Sharon and the screws. 'Nice dress, Kate,' they said. Thanks. Bloody Bo Peep! He's a real sod at times, my husband.

I thanked the catering manager. He'd really done us proud. The food was wonderful and in the centre of the table as decoration they'd placed an amazing dolphin all carved in ice. The champagne went down well, too.

Officially, as patients, Ron and Charlie were only allowed one glass of champagne each, but Ron would drink half of his then one of his mates, or me, would pour ours into his so he was never with out a full glass.

Ron was talking business as usual and he had relaxed, so I dashed up to Ron, the photographer, and said: 'Quick, take the photos now while he's in the mood.' Ron doesn't like having his picture taken and he doesn't like a lot of fuss, but I made him stand in front of a white wall. I didn't want those awful curtains in the picture or those bars.

But by now he was scowling. Ron hates being told what to do or where to stand. Good old Joey Pyle came to the rescue.

'Oi, Ron!' he said. 'Nipper Read's dead!' And Ron started laughing. So now those are the only pictures I've got where Ron doesn't look all menacing.

'Go on Ron, kiss me, kiss me,' I laughed and they were saying: 'Go on Ron!'

So we kissed for the camera, although it was difficult really because we were laughing so much. He put his arms around me and together we cut the pink-and-white cake. It was great fun, lovely. But I knew it had to end soon.

'Sorry Kate,' said one of the screws. 'It's time to go now.' For a short while we'd forgotten where we were – but not for long. They told us all to wait. Before anyone left they wanted to count all the plates and the knives and forks to make sure none had been nicked!

I stood with Ron as he said goodbye to our guests. They were all choked. They didn't want to leave him and neither did I. One by one they hugged him, shook his hand. 'See you Ron, take it easy.'

Then I had to go. I felt as if I was abandoning him and I was a bit upset. Ron gave me a kiss and a cuddle. 'Go on,' he said softly. 'Go on and have a good time.' It didn't seem right, but I knew all the other guests would be at the Hilton by now and Ron wanted me to celebrate with them.

As Reggie always says to me: 'Remember Kate, you're Ron's ambassador now.' And from that moment I suppose I was.

The gates slammed shut behind us as we sped off in the Rolls. It still hadn't sunk in. I felt as if I was an actress in a film and just being swept along by the plot. Everything was happening so fast. I was happy, but I was sad that I wasn't with Ron. I was tired but I was on a high – adrenalin was keeping me going.

The photographers hadn't gone, and so we had to fight our way through the hotel reception until one of Ron's friends told them all: 'Get back, boys, get back.' And they did. They agreed that if I'd pose for one picture they'd go away and leave us alone. So I posed with my new brother-in-law, Charlie Kray, and then we went into the room where all two hundred guests were waiting to meet me.

I felt a bit lost. Who were all these people? I couldn't see a face I knew. But then, in the crowd, I saw Harry-boy's smiling face and there was Sharon and Ron's friends who'd been at the ceremony and they looked after me.

People kept coming up to congratulate me. 'I'm so and so, give my regards to the Colonel.'

I had messages from Ron to give to some of them and I thanked God I had a good memory.

'I'm so and so,' a man would say.

'Oh, hello, Ron says can you go up and visit him on Thursday.'

'I'm John. Congratulations.'

'Thanks. And Ron says can you get in touch. He wants a word.'

At eight o'clock, I slipped away to my room and rang Ron, as I always did. I wasn't allowed to speak to him in those days, but I always rang to say that everything was OK and goodnight.

'Hey Ron, it's your missus on the phone,' said the screw as I gave him the message, and in the background I could hear Ron laugh. They'd allowed him to take one tier of the cake and some of the left-over food back to his ward so he was having a bit of a celebration with his friends there. That made me feel better. At least he wasn't on his own.

'Tell him everything's going well; we're all having a good time and I'll see him tomorrow.'

Back at the party everyone was enjoying themselves. Of course there was hardly a woman in sight. A few guests had brought their wives, but not many. Mostly it was big men in big suits, men from all over the country – Scotland and the Midlands, Cardiff and, of course, London. They'd all come to show their respect for Ron.

The hotel had hired a pianist for us, so, while the waitresses handed around the food, he played quietly in the background. I was steered around by Charlie and tried desperately to remember all the names and faces. But dancing? You've got to be joking! These men don't dance – they just stand at the bar talking business. Business first – everything else second.

At first Ron said he didn't want pictures taken at the party, but then someone decided it would be nice for Ron to have a memento of the occasion – and also for him to see who had turned up. It would have been a liberty if some people hadn't!

So I've got a pile of photos from the party. And I'm not the only one, I bet. As I was travelling through the room I'd say to one of Ron's friends: 'Who's that?'

And they'd say: 'That's the Old Bill.' There were quite a few plain-clothes policemen milling around – gate-crashers, I might add – who were taking note of the faces that were there. Bloody cheek!

One by one Ron's friends came up to say goodbye. 'Give my love to the Colonel.' Or: 'Give my love to your old man.' Some were going back home, some were staying at the hotel and others invited me to go on to a club. But I didn't want to go. I had to be up early anyway to see Ron.

I went up to my room alone. It was full of cards – we got hundreds of them from people in Broadmoor, from friends and family and from people who just like and respect the Krays. There were flowers, too, but not my bouquet of roses. I'd given that to Charlie to put on their mum's grave. Ron never asked me to, but I just thought it was the right thing to do. We both wished she'd been alive to be at the wedding.

The room was a mess and cluttered, but there weren't any wedding presents. I mean, what were people going to give us – a toaster? We did get some cutlery, but Ron told everyone to give us individual gifts if anything at all.

It was one o'clock in the morning and I was absolutely knackered. I was too tired even for a cup of tea. I pulled off my wedding dress and put it on the chair and put on my wedding-night lingerie – a big old blue t-shirt!

I moved all the silver horseshoes and good-luck charms I'd been given off the bed and sank in between the sheets. Ugh! Sharon had obviously been up to the room. The bed was full of confetti, which stuck to my bum. But I didn't care and it made me smile.

As soon as I closed my eyes I was gone. That first night as Mrs Ronald Kray, I slept like a log.

## CHAPTER TWO

# *Life Before Ron*

'Which one are you married to?'

'Ron,' I say.

'Which one's gay?'

'Ron.'

'Which one's in the nut-house?'

'Ron.'

At this point there's always an embarrassed pause. Then they look at me and say: 'Why did you marry him?'

It's the million-dollar question, the one everyone asks – or at least wants to. I'm only thirty-seven, blonde, a size twelve and I always make the effort to look good even if I'm just going down the shops. I'm not beautiful – but I don't look like the back end of a bus, either! So people always seem to be surprised when they meet me.

I can read their minds: 'What's a girl like you doing married to one of the most notorious gangsters in British history, a man who suffers from paranoid schizophrenia, who killed a man, who's locked up in a hospital for the criminally insane, who's bisexual and twenty-three years older to boot?'

Before Ron and me got married, I had to visit Mr Franey, the Governor of Broadmoor, and Dr Ferris, who was then Ron's doctor there, and those are the very same questions they asked, too. But I wasn't scared to answer. I wasn't at all nervous of meeting them and talking about it. I knew I was doing the right thing and I didn't feel I had anything to prove.

But I didn't blame them for asking those questions. Ron had been married before in Broadmoor, to a very nice lady called Elaine. It all came out later that one of the reasons Ron had done it was that a newspaper thought it would be a good story, and they'd paid Elaine a bit of money!

I knew this was different between Ron and me, but I could understand that the people who look after Ron at Broadmoor had to be sure. They had to be convinced, as much as anyone could be, that I wasn't going to swan in, marry Ron and swan off again. Apart from the publicity and things like that, Ron's well-being had to be their first priority. He is, after all, in their care.

They told me I'd made a big difference to Ron's life. Of course his basic character hadn't changed – I couldn't change a man like Ron and, anyway, I wouldn't want to. But everyone around him – the screws, the doctors, the people who knew him best – said he'd seemed happier since I'd been around. I suppose I cheered him up. Before, Ron was a bit quiet and didn't trust a lot of people and he always saw the serious side of things. Now the staff on the ward said he found it much easier to laugh at life and I was well pleased to hear that.

But they said they had to be sure. Was this really what Ron wanted? Was it what I wanted? And why? They were very blunt about it. Was I marrying him because he was famous, because he was a name?

No, I wasn't. If I wanted someone just because he was famous I could probably go out to a London club and find someone equally famous – and someone who was younger and not gay and who'd be around outside to look after me!

Was I marrying him for money? No. That's a joke. Ron doesn't have much money, and if he does get any he gives it away. Anyway, he's not exactly in regular employment, is he? Ron doesn't keep me now and never has, and at the time we were married I was running two companies, I had a Rolls-Royce and three properties so why would I marry a man like Ron? He is probably the most generous man I've ever met and he'll give me money if I need it if – and it's a big if – he's got it. But I support myself.

So why was I marrying him, then? It's not an easy question. Ask any married person exactly why they got married and I bet, if they're honest, they'd have to think about it. It's such a personal question, and the only people who can really answer are the people involved – and even then they probably don't understand the half of it.

Why? they asked me. Because I love him, I said. Because he's special, different. Because I wanted to. Because he wanted me to. Because I knew, like you know really deep down sometimes, that it was the right thing to do. You don't know why or how you know, you just do.

All that is true. But now, looking back, I can say it wasn't and isn't as simple as that.

They also wanted to know if I knew what I was letting myself in for. Oh yes, I said cheerfully. But I was wrong. I didn't. Not really. Four years later, I don't regret marrying Ron, not for a single moment, and everything I said is still true. The basic reason I married him is because I loved him and I still love him, more now than I did then, if anything.

But all the things that have happened to me since have made me ask myself the question everyone else seems to want answered and I now realize, after a lot of painful thinking, that love wasn't the only reason. Nice if it was – but nothing in life is as straightforward as that.

Maybe it's all a question of being in the right – or wrong – place, meeting the right – or wrong – person at the right – or wrong – time. So much of life is chance and to come close to understanding why I married Ron you have to understand something of my life before I met him.

Just like I knew it was the right thing to marry Ron, I always knew from a very young age that during my life I would somehow be involved with the prison service. It might sound crazy and, of course, things didn't turn out quite as I expected they would, but in a way you have to admit that premonition came true, didn't it?!

When I was younger, I applied to be a prison officer. They turned me down. Then I applied to be a traffic warden. But they turned me down too. Hardly surprising, really. The snag came when they asked on the application forms if me or any of my family had any criminal convictions.

Well, I've never been inside in my life, thank God, but... my auntie went away for stabbing someone with a knitting needle, then there were my uncles who were a bit naughty at times, and my brother – he went away – and a cousin or two – they went away, and I can remember my younger brother Tony being dragged away as a kid to Borstal screaming his head off. They all went away as I was growing up – just for little things like demanding money with menaces which, if you knew the circumstances, wasn't nearly as bad as it sounds!

My mum used to be furious when any of us kids got into trouble and she'd give whoever was responsible a damn good belt. We went to visit one of our young uncles once, after he was sent away to a children's home for some little misdemeanour or other and we felt really sorry for him – until we saw him. The kids at this place were all clean and they had nice clothes. They even had a big climbing frame that my uncle used to climb all over. He seemed to be having the time of his life, so the rest of us didn't feel too sorry for him after that.

We all lived in my Nan's boarding house at 5 London Road, Swanscombe, a small town in Kent which is known locally as the Holy City, where all the women are supposed to be born with beautiful skin because of the special water you find there.

The boarding house was a tall, thin, dirty-looking terraced place and in those days it was an absolute madhouse.

My dad's Irish and he and his brother had come over from Cork to work at the Blue Circle cement works opposite. They lodged at Nan's and they both ended up staying. My dad got my mum pregnant – he was a bit of a scoundrel in those days and he's always had an eye for the ladies! She was only fifteen, and they've been together ever since.

His brother married my mum's sister, and they went and lived up the road. But Mum and Dad stayed at Nan's and they had four children: Joe, he's the sensible one; then me, my brother Tony and my young sister Maggie. But Nan was still young and she was still having kids at the same time as my mum was producing hers, and Nan had thirteen in all. So there were four grown-ups and seventeen of us kids all living together. That's what I mean by a madhouse!

It was bloody chaos at times. Us kids all used to sleep in these great big beds – girls together and boys together – and Tony used to catch the bedbugs, squash them against the wall and then proudly circle them with a pen.

Grandad worked in the cement factory, and I remember going to the Blue Circle works dos with my brothers and sister and uncles and aunties and cousins, and we all had to wear name tags on our buttons because there were so many of us. The West kids, that's what they called us.

Dad was working, too, as a steeplejack. He used to build those big chimneys. He even did the Post Office Tower. He was foreman there and he used to take us young ones up on the train to look at it.

But there wasn't much money coming in, barely enough to manage with so many kids. It was years before I knew you were supposed to have milk with cornflakes – we always had them with hot water. Now I like them better that way!

And it wasn't until I was older and visited other kids that I realized that most people didn't lock up their food. Mum used to lock up all our food in a big cupboard with a huge padlock so we didn't scoff the lot. Going down the chippy was a major expedition. Two of us kids had to go because one couldn't carry it all. We'd get a pennyworth of chips and some crackling for all the kids, fish and chips for the grown-ups, then on the way back Tony and me would stop down an alley and stuff our faces before we got back to the house.

Just like in Ron's family, the women were the strong ones. Like Ron, my dad is quietly-spoken and he's kept his Irish accent. Grandad was a skinny little man, and he always seemed to be asleep. He'd sit there in an armchair in the kitchen snoring his head off and Nan would flick him with a tea towel to wake him up. She was a big woman, who always wore a pinny, and I never once saw her outside the house. She'd go out in the yard to hang up her washing but that was it. The only time she ventured further afield was when the council moved us all from the boarding house into two houses opposite each other up the road. And even then she just got in a car one end and out of it the other.

Dad was gentle and never once lifted a hand to us, but Mum used to bash us about at times. I was a bit frightened of her then. I think we all were. But, looking back, it can't have been an easy life. She had four kids before she was twenty and there were all her brothers and sisters to take care of, too.

She also suffered terribly from PMT and once a month she'd go absolutely crazy. Tony got the worst of it. She'd hit him with anything she could lay her hands on – fire tongs, sticks, you name it. But Tony's always been a bit wild. He'd raid the gas meters, pinch our Post Office books, and he once chopped the arms off my favourite green checked Ben Sherman shirt because I wouldn't lend it to him!

We all went to school together and I used to fight with the boys all the time. My Mum's half-caste and, although

I'm one of the fairest in the family, a lot of us are quite dark and some of the other children used to call us the 'woggy West kids'. Someone would make a crack about one of my uncles and I used to put them right and give them a good smack.

I suppose I liked having all my brothers and uncles around to protect me but, underneath all the larking about, I wasn't happy. We didn't have a lot as kids and although that's not supposed to matter it does sometimes. I was very jealous of my best friend Annie, a nice girl with lovely long blonde hair. She used to have birthday parties and then she always got a green jelly made in a mould shaped like a rabbit. I've never had a birthday party in my life, and I've always wanted one with a green-rabbit jelly!

There's a lot of old cobblers talked about big families, as if it's all sweetness and light all the time. It's not. Often there's a darker side. I was only seven when I was molested by one of my cousins. He was a bit weird. I remember thinking he was very old, but he was probably only about twenty-five at the time and he said he was going to take me and my brother to the fair.

But he didn't. He took us to some waste ground and made Tony stand a little way away in the bushes. Then he grabbed me. 'You should never come down here on your own,' he said, 'cos men will want to grab you.'

I didn't know what he was talking about.

'I'll show you what they do and I'll give you half a crown if you don't tell anybody.' He grabbed me between my legs and pushed me to the ground. The ground was hard and the stones and gorse scratched my bare legs. I didn't know what he was up to, but I knew I didn't like it.

I managed to struggle up and started screaming and crying. I got Tony by the hand and we ran away as fast as we could. A little while later I found out he'd been sent to prison for raping a little girl, so maybe I had a lucky escape.

If something like that happens to you as a child you never forget it. You remember the details so clearly it's like putting on a video and you're back there. I can still see his horrible face close to mine. I've never spoken to him since.

Years later, when I was twenty, it happened again and this time it was worse, much worse. And again it was someone in the family. They say it's always someone you know and trust and that's what makes incest the worst abuse of all. You're so muddled up because you love that person and you don't want to stop loving them, but you're frightened of them too because you know what they've tried to do.

I still see the man who abused me the second time and I don't hate him. He cried afterwards. I can still picture him with tears running down his face and that was awful. I still love him; you can't stop loving just like that. But I don't trust him any more and that's a terrible thing to feel about one of your family.

Now people talk a lot about child abuse, as if it's only just started happening. But it's always gone on and probably often in big families. Although I didn't realize it at the time, I wasn't the only victim. Last year my sister Maggie told me she'd been molested too, by one of our family when she was little. We were decorating my flat when suddenly she blurted out: 'I haven't ever told you this before . . .' And then she told me how he used to touch her up and make her do things to him. I was shocked. I'd always thought this man was great; when I was a kid I thought he was brilliant and he'd never touched me.

I think what happened to Maggie really had a bad effect on her – she's never had much confidence as a result of it. She says she doesn't want to kill the bastard – she's far too frightened of him – but she'll never see him again. I always used to wonder why she never mentioned his name, but I never asked. Perhaps I should have done – perhaps that's the secret. We shouldn't just wonder, we should always ask. Because neither Maggie or I told anyone at the time what had happened to us. We were both too scared.

The effect it all had on me was to make me a bit wary of men I didn't know – and of some I did. You become very aware of danger. There's no way you'd ever catch me in a train compartment alone with a man. I'd rather get off and wait for the next train. So I'm late, so what? I'm safe.

But I don't feel that what happened influenced my relationships with men when I grew up. Maybe a psychiatrist would disagree, but I've always liked men, got on with men. And, even after that awful time when I was seven, I still grew up with a healthy interest in the opposite sex!

I met both my first two husbands when I was eleven. Andy was a hippie type who wore a big smelly sheepskin coat and he was handsome, too, with long, blonde hair. Then there was Harry, another boy in Andy's school.

Harry was a bit younger but he had a hairy chest when

he was eleven! He was a real dude, a cut above the rest, and he always seemed to have loads of money. Even then Harry had his clothes made up in town and he was really flash. He was smart as well, although not always that smart – he was done for possessing speed when he was just fourteen.

I kept a photo of Harry in my bra even though I was going out with Andy. Harry was just so special, but he wasn't interested in me – I was far too unsophisticated!

Andy and I started sleeping together when I was thirteen. I used to go to his house almost every day. It was on a council estate, but I thought it was really posh. They used to have a proper dinner. His mum would cook and they'd all sit down at the table – very different from home, where we hardly ever sat down together and you were lucky if Nan cooked egg and chips!

Andy's dad had only one arm, but he still managed to run his own driving school, although what people thought when he got in the car armless I can't imagine! He took me out for a lesson once, but I crashed his car into a tree so it was no more lessons for me! I remember he used to come in from work, take his arm off and put it in the airing cupboard!

They were a funny family and they never thought I was good enough for Andy. Even when we were married they used to make me come in the back door.

When I was fifteen, I got pregnant and Andy's mum was livid. When we told her she just turned around and told me to get rid of it. Then I had to tell my mum. I was dreading it. I waited until she was alone in the kitchen.

'Mum, I've got some thing to tell you.'

'What?'

'I'm pregnant.'

BOSH! She knocked me right across the kitchen. But she still came with me when I went for the abortion. It was 1971, and abortion had just been legalized, but in those days you still had to have a really good excuse to get one and several doctors had to sign their agreement.

First we went to our GP, a horrible man who looked at me as if I was a real slag. Then we got the bus to Dartford hospital, me with tears streaming down my face. I wanted the baby. I didn't want this abortion, but I knew I had no choice.

They did it and I woke up, looked down at myself and there was blood all over the sheets. I was terrified. I'd been about five months gone because I'd been too scared to tell anyone about it and I remember the nursing staff telling me quite coldly that the baby had been a boy.

It wasn't long after I came out of hospital that I started to feel sick, really sick. I was losing blood and I went to Andy's house to get help. As soon as I arrived I felt I had to go up to the toilet. I sat on the toilet and put my hand down and then I was screaming. A little baby's arm came out of me.

Andy's dad rushed upstairs and when Andy and his mum came back from work he showed it to them. Dear God, a complete arm and hand, but putrefied. Then he threw it on the fire. I'll never forget that as long as I live. He threw it on the fire. I collapsed and they called an ambulance which took me back to hospital. It turned out they'd really botched the abortion, they hadn't taken all the baby away and I had peritonitis.

It took a long time for me to get over that, but Andy and I stayed together and just before my eighteenth birthday, on 1 June 1974, we got married. We had a white wedding with all the trimmings and I looked the part of the young, blushing bride in a long white dress, white veil, white gloves and carrying a white parasol and a bouquet of red roses.

The wedding was great but the marriage was a farce.

Andy was my first love, but we should never have got married. Two weeks after the wedding I was seeing another bloke.

We lived at Andy's mum's, and one day I came home – through the back door of course – and there was Andy, my eighteen-year-old husband, sitting at the kitchen table, in his pink-striped pyjamas, smoking a pipe.

It was like being struck by lightning. I looked at him and then I looked again and then I thought: 'My God, is this what the rest of my life is going to be like?'

Not long afterwards it was our first anniversary and I walked in the back door straight into a surprise party. There they all were: Andy, his mum and dad, aunties and uncles. 'Happy anniversary, Kate!'

I looked around. 'Where's my mum and dad and my family?'

'Oh, we didn't invite them.'

So I told them all what I thought of them. They really believed they were too good for my mum and dad and that was wrong. Andy tried to make the peace and handed me a bunch of a dozen red roses, but I didn't want them. I whacked him around the neck with them and red petals flew everywhere!

The next day, a year and a day after my wedding, I took my things and left and I haven't seen Andy or his family since. He's probably still living at home with his mum, still smoking his pipe and still wearing his pink pyjamas. I saw a shirt I liked in a shop in the High Street, so I flogged my wedding ring and bought it and that was well and truly that.

I went back home and knocked on the door. Mum answered and I told her I'd left Andy. She told me to piss off. I'd made my bed so I could bloody well lie in it.

So I went to live with my brother Joe in his flat, and for a while he put up with me, although God knows why. Freedom went straight to my head and I was wild. It was a mad time. I'd left school at fourteen and my first job was working as an office girl in a London underwear factory. But it was boring and the boss sang 'Little Green Apples' all day, which drove me right around the bend.

So I'd left there and now I was working down at my mum's paper factory. This was much more fun, and me and the other girls used to get up to all sorts.

Then I fell in love with someone I thought was really gorgeous – handsome and, at thirty, quite a lot older than me. But he wasn't gorgeous at all. He was lowlife. He was also married. His wife was pregnant when he was seeing me and when I got pregnant too he didn't want to know. 'Get rid of it,' he said, so, like a fool, I went and had another abortion. And they botched it up again. And I was ill again.

After I came out of hospital I was walking along the road when he drove past, the bastard.

He stopped the car. 'You had it done, then?' he said.

'Yes,' I said and carried on walking.

He opened the car door. 'Well, hop in then.'

As if I'd go with him after that. So I told him to fuck off and that was the end of him.

It wasn't a happy time. I started drinking really heavily – Pernod and blackcurrant was my favourite tipple and now even the smell of aniseed makes me feel ill. I started seeing another chap who lived nearby and we had a mad affair.

It wasn't so much passionate as drunken, and he'd knock me about a bit. But even so, when we finished, I got the needle and I was determined to get my own back. So, one day when he was out, I broke into his house and I was looking around at all the things I could do to annoy him – like chopping the arms off all his shirts!

And then I saw them – his prize budgies which he kept in an aviary in the kitchen. 'I know,' I thought, 'I'll liberate his bleeding budgies – that'll teach him!' I had visions of him coming back and leaping around the kitchen trying to catch his birds.

So I let them out, and they flapped about a bit and I left. Next day the chap came home and all six of them were there, in the washing-up bowl in the sink – drowned. It even made the local paper – 'INTRUDER BREAKS IN AND DROWNS BUDGIES.' But I would like to say here and now that I never drowned those budgies. No one believes me. Even now, every now and then, my friends say: 'Go on, Kate. Come clean. You did do them budgies, didn't you?' And when I told Ron he thought it was the funniest thing he'd ever heard and said: 'You did it, didn't you?'

But I didn't. I think what must have happened was that

they were all flying about and they wanted a drink, so they went and perched on the washing-up bowl and then they all fell in. I never drowned them. Honest, cross my heart!

It was a bad time for budgies, and bad for me, too. I was in a terrible state. I knew Joe was worried about my drinking, but I didn't care. Then one day I was in his flat, sitting on the sofa pissed out of my brain. I felt so sick that Joe brought me a bucket. I was sick into it, but I must have put my head so far in that when I sat up it was still on my head and there was vomit running all down my hair, all over my clothes. I'd sunk about as low as I could go.

Joe went and got his camera and took a Polaroid picture of me – looking like that. The next day when I'd sobered up he showed it to me. He said: 'Look, Kate. Go on, look. Look at yourself. This is you. This is what's happened to you and this is what you look like.'

I just burst into tears. I looked terrible. And since that day, apart from the occasional glass of champagne, I haven't touched a drop of alcohol. I don't drink.

Understandably, Joe wanted me out and Dad came and got me. Dad also went and sorted out the chap who'd been bashing me about. He didn't make a fuss about it. He just quietly went and knocked out all of his front teeth and told him to keep away from me! I was very proud of my dad for that – I love my dad.

Things got a bit better after that, but I didn't feel life was taking me anywhere. All the rest of the family seemed happy enough to stay in Swanscombe, but I wasn't. I wanted out. I wanted to escape. I wanted more – but I wasn't quite sure what.

Then I met Harry again. I used to knock around with a girl called Mandy and we had a right laugh. One day we went up to a place called the Nelson in Gravesend where everyone used to go. And there he was standing by the bar – Harry, still in his lovely suits, still flash.

He was talking to this bird, but he left her standing and came over to me. I told him about being molested by one of the family and the next day he suggested I move in with him. I said yes straight away. Meeting Harry again was the best thing that had happened to me in a very long time.

A year later we got married. I booked it up at the registry office and just Harry and me went down there in a cab and then home for fish and chips.

I was madly in love with Harry and he was in love with me and it was wonderful. For the first time in my life I had someone who really loved me, who was really good to me, who took care of me. How can I describe Harry? Everyone loves Harry – I don't know anyone who doesn't like Harry. He's a smashing man, just so comical with this dry sense of humour. A good man.

It was a very happy time. Harry was working for a builders, scaffolding, and I worked as a lifeguard at the local swimming pool in Gravesend. He encouraged me to take exams and better my qualifications and I'd say: 'I can't take these exams, I'm not clever enough.'

But Harry would say: 'Yes, you are. Go for it. You can do anything you like.' So I took the exams and became a swimming instructor.

You can talk to Harry about anything, anything at all. He gave me confidence when I didn't have any.

At one time I had a funny phobia about eating in front of other people. But Harry helped me over that and other things too.

If I said: 'I fancy doing this or that but I can't,' he'd turn round and say: 'Go on, do it. You can do it. If you fail it doesn't matter; at least you've had a go.'

We moved from a little flat into a bigger one and then into a lovely big house in the country at Benenden near the posh girls' school. At least Harry loved the house; I thought it was spooky, and the neighbours were snobby. I was walking down our drive one day and there was our next-door neighbour in his garden.

I went: 'Hi-ya!'

He stopped his digging and raised his snooty nose at me. 'I'm sorry?' he said.

'I said "Hi-ya!"'

'I'm sorry,' he said. 'I thought you were speaking some kind of Gaelic!'

But just because they were posh didn't mean they were all as squeaky-clean as they liked to make out. Harry and I were running a second-hand-clothes shop called Flash Harry's in Maidstone at the time and we'd also just started our kissagram business.

One day I took the order for a schoolgirl kissagram at a really posh house just down the road from us. Off I trotted in my St Trinian's uniform, stockings and suspenders, and I did all the usual stuff – posed for pictures, sang 'Happy Birthday' and gave Birthday Boy a kiss. Then just as I was leaving this old geezer sidled up to me looking a bit shifty.

'Could I put on your shoe?' he said.

'You what?'

'Please,' he whispered. 'Please let me.'

'Get away,' I said and 'silly old sod'. I thought. But if it makes him happy, well, who cares? So I took off my shoe and gave it to him and he sniffed it! Then there he was trying to get his great fat foot into it. He couldn't, of course. I only take a size three!

Harry and I had a good laugh about it afterwards, but I thought no more about it until we went to the village summer fête on the vicarage lawn. And there he was – the shoe man – standing there, looking all smart in a suit and shaking hands with all the posh ladies in their flowery hats! I couldn't resist it – I went up to him.

'Hello,' I said.

He went quite white. 'Oh my God,' he said, 'don't tell anyone. Don't say anything...' As if I would!

The kissagram business was hard work but great fun, and we made quite a bit of money too. Harry chauffeured me around. I'd be dressed as a schoolgirl, or a woman police officer or traffic warden or sometimes topless in just a pretty silk basque, stockings and suspenders. Being topless never bothered me. It was all harmless fun and the men never pawed me. They all stuck to the rule: look but don't touch and, anyway, I had Harry with me in case they got any funny ideas.

It was a laugh. I even roped in my poor old brother, Joe, to do a few and you'd see him whizzing round Kent on his bike in his gorilla suit or his policeman's gear. I made him a Superman costume. He complained it was so tight he couldn't get it off. Once he was doing a party at a pub, and when he left he found he'd locked the car with the keys inside. So he went back inside and asked if anyone could open the car door.

'Well, you're bloody Superman,' they said. 'You open it!' Unfortunately, not everyone was so easy-going. Once Joe was set upon by a load of drunken hooligans who threw him in the river and broke his leg. He was dressed as Tarzan at the time!

They were happy times, but for Harry and me there was sadness, too. Harry and I always wanted kids and we started trying as soon as we got married. Nothing happened. I was in and out of hospital. I lost count of the times I went in for this test or that.

They found that after the two botched abortions my insides were damaged, so I had an operation. But still nothing happened and they suggested IVF.

We went to Bourne Hall in Cambridge, where the first test-tube baby had been born. It's one of the top clinics in the country, an amazing place, but it didn't work for us, just like it doesn't work for four out of five couples.

I was desperately upset. So was Harry. He was wonderful to me, great, but it was heartbreaking. Unless you've been through it, you don't really understand how awful it is – all the hoping, then all the disappointment.

We tried for adoption and they showed us a book full of pictures of poor little handicapped kids, but we knew we didn't really want that. You have to be honest with yourself.

So we tried IVF again and again it didn't work, and this time I lay flat on my back for a month after the treatment praying for a baby. They said I should try again in a year, and I kept telling myself that during that year I would get strong enough to go through it all again, but I knew I couldn't face it. I just couldn't.

Harry was brilliant, but I was so depressed even he couldn't help me. They say having treatment for infertility brings couples together. That's not always true. Sometimes the strain of it tears you apart, and soon without even consciously realizing it we began to drift in opposite directions.

It was more my fault than his – I pulled away from him. I still hoped that maybe I would have a baby one day, one day. My head knew it was hopeless, but in your heart you go on clinging to a little bit of hope.

Every woman yearns for a baby, and there are still times when I could just throw myself off a bridge, the yearning is so much. Every time I see a baby, every time I hold a little one, it's there, that yearning. It never goes away.

And people are so cruel and insensitive. 'Oh, I wish I was like you,' women say to me, and them with two or three lovely kids. 'All that time to yourself, that freedom. If I had my time over again...'

But it's crap. They don't mean it, and I feel like getting them by the throat and saying, 'Don't fucking patronize me.'

For me and Harry it was the end of the road. It's difficult to put into words, but after that there was nothing left of our marriage. I love Harry and he loves me, but I'm not in love with him and he's not in love with me.

Perhaps if we'd stayed in love and had a family it all might have been different. But what do you do after ten years of trying to have a baby? There's nothing left, nowhere to go.

I was very depressed. I felt terribly guilty about the abortions – both baby boys, they'd told me. Maybe I blamed Harry too, a little bit. That's totally unfair but you don't always think logically about things like this. Maybe he blamed me, I don't know. I don't think so – he's too nice a person.

After thirteen years together we parted. If we'd stayed together we'd have ended up hating each other and neither of us could have borne that.

In a way, after so long trying to have a baby together and failing, I wanted to cut off from everything that had been part of that part of my life. And that included Harry.

It was a strange time. I was in limbo, waiting for something to happen. I wanted to change my life. I wanted something different. I wanted more, I wanted...I didn't know what I wanted.

And then I met the twins.

## CHAPTER THREE

# *Meeting the Family*

I don't scare easily, and it wasn't as if I'd never visited anyone in prison before, but one look at Gartree top-security prison outside Leicester and I was a bundle of nerves. It's so grey and bleak, a huge old prison standing there in the middle of huge cornfields. Gartree looks serious. And what was I going to say to this man? Should I kiss him on the cheek, shake his hand or what? I'd never met him – I hardly knew him.

Given half a chance I would have turned on my heel and left. But I'd promised Reggie Kray I'd visit him and I wasn't going to let him down. One thing I had learned is how much people inside look forward to their visits – and how disappointed they are when people don't show up or are late.

Looking back, everything about my relationship with Ron, how we met and married, seems somehow to have been meant. Fate, if you like.

Ron has always had a strong belief in God. When he was younger, he said it was like a constant battle going on inside him – the good and the bad always pulling and pushing him in different directions. He's also a firm believer in an afterlife, and he knows that his mum Violet is always looking after him from the other side. He says his mum sent me to him. Maybe that's true; I don't know. But the way it all happened made me feel that I was walking into something, towards something, I was being led along and it was as if I didn't have a choice about it.

I was thirty-two, my marriage to Harry was over and my dreams of having a baby too. I was drifting, unsure where to go or what to do next. I'd heard of the Krays, of course – who hasn't – but I'd never really given them much thought. Why should I?

After all, I was only thirteen when they were put away.

One day I was standing in Charing Cross station after a shopping trip in London. I was feeling pretty miffed because I'd just missed my train, so I was skulking about the bookshop waiting for the next one to come along when I saw a book about the Krays called *The Profession of Violence* by John Pearson. It had David Bailey's famous 1960s photo of Reg and Ron on the cover. It was the first time I'd ever seen a picture of them.

On the spur of the moment I bought it and spent the journey home reading it. When I'd finished it I was intrigued and curious, and I did something I'd never done before – I got out pen and paper to write a letter to someone I'd never met: Reggie Kray. I wasn't sure what to put in it so I wrote this jokey letter asking Reg if he was going grey around the Shirleys and still had all his own teeth! I didn't expect a letter in return and I was really made up when I got a reply on my birthday.

Reggie's a wonderful letter writer; he's got a lovely way with words, and after we'd exhanged a letter or two he phoned me. I picked up the phone and a voice said: 'Hello, Reggie Kray here...' I found out later he always starts his calls like that and I wasn't the first or the last person to be struck immediately speechless! I was sure it was somebody larking about, but how could it be? No one knew I was writing to him.

Reg asked me to visit and I couldn't say no. Anyway, by this time, I was curious to meet him. So, as soon as he could get a visit, I put on my best grey silk suit and drove up to Leicester.

Security at Gartree is tight and I defy anyone not to feel nervous as they search you and your bag and make you walk through a metal detector. Then there's the way they lock all the heavy doors after you as they lead you to the visiting room. It's a horrible experience, but it makes you realize how the prisoners must feel when they first arrive and it sinks in that those doors aren't going to be unlocked for years and years.

Everyone else on a visit went into a big hall, but an officer came up to me and said: 'Mr Kray has asked to see you in the private room at the end of the hall,' and I could sense the other visitors staring at me and nudging each other. I was shown into a tiny room with just one table and two chairs. I came in one door and Reggie came in the other. We sat down and there were all these screws watching us from outside the door. I was really nervous.

'Shut that door,' said Reggie.

'You sound just like Everard!' I said, and he did, just like Larry Grayson in the TV programme.

He burst out laughing. We hit it off straight away. I really liked him, but he was nothing like I'd expected. I'd pictured Reggie as massive, all broad and bolshie and maybe a bit of a big-head. But he's nothing like that. He's quite small, really energetic and very trendy. He may have been away for a long time, but Reggie loves music, he knows what's what, he's got a fashionable haircut and most of the time he wears jeans, a sweatshirt and Reebok trainers. You can also see that he makes the effort to keep fit. He looks good.

Before long, we were chatting away as if we'd known each other all our lives. I made him laugh. He said he'd never had letters like mine and yes, he was going grey around the temples and yes, he did have all his own teeth!

First we discussed business. It's always business first with the twins. The first thing either of them will say to you on the phone or when you meet them is, 'Got any news?' It's always, 'Got any news?' before you've even had a chance to say hello. They hunger for news of outside.

Then there are messages to pass on, and then they'll say: 'Now, could you ring so and so for me' or 'Could you ask so and so to do such and such?' And I sit there like a secretary taking it all down.

But after we'd finished the business, Reggie and I chatted away. He said he'd never met anyone like me before . . . and I must meet Ron.

One of the first things you discover when you meet Reggie or Ron is how close they still are. It doesn't matter that it's been years since they lived together, it makes no difference that they're in separate prisons hundreds of miles apart. I don't think it would change anything if one was here and the other was in Australia. Nobody and nothing can break the incredible bond between the twins.

Once you've met one he always wants you to meet the other. Reggie and Ron write to each other every day, sometimes twice or three times a day. Ron will write only occasionally to anyone else – and then only if it's business or to me – but letters to Reggie are different.

So they're in touch every day and they put as much as they can into their letters. But everything they write is censored – even now, if Ron ever writes to me there's always a blue slip saying the letter has been read by the authorities. It's understandable, I suppose, but it doesn't make for much privacy between husband and wife.

If there are things they don't want the screws to read, they'll send messages to each other through their visitors and once every three months Reg is driven down from whichever prison he's in to see Ron at Broadmoor. He stays for the ten-to-twelve visit and the two-to-four visit, and they're allowed to have lunch together.

Reg gets the usual slop food in prison, but Ron is allowed decent food and I can send things in, so he'll say, 'Reg is coming, get in something decent.' And then I'll order some lobsters and prawns for them, so it's a proper occasion.

Of course, it doesn't always turn out as planned. Like most brothers they have their rucks – except theirs are usually long-distance rucks and often carried on by letter. They have an argument in one letter and make it up in the next. And occasionally Reggie makes the long journey to Broadmoor, and they've been carrying on one of their rows by letter, and when they meet, they have a quick row, Ron says, 'Fuck off!' and Reggie does. Or vice versa.

But you'll never hear one twin say a word against the other and, if they do make any money from a book or a film, it's always cut straight down the middle. Everything is always fifty per cent to Ron, fifty per cent to Reg.

Neither is the boss. People are always asking me, 'Who's the boss, Ron or Reg?' Reggie is the elder – by ten minutes – but it isn't like that. If Ron puts his foot down about something, Reggie will let him get away with it, but another time it's the other way around and Ron will give in to Reg.

I think Reggie is a little more tolerant than Ron, a bit more flexible. Reggie might let a friend take a liberty, but if they took a liberty with Ron that would be that. No one would dare with Ron; Ron won't stand nonsense from anyone.

To an outsider, the bond between the twins is extraordinary but if you love either of them you have to accept from the start that it's Ron and Reg, Reg and Ron. It's always been like that and it always will be.

Even if one of them is sending a birthday card, he'd never sign it with just his name alone. It's always Ron and Reg. Their telepathy is incredibly powerful. More than once I've been speaking to Reg on the phone and he's said: 'What's the matter with Ron?' Nothing, I say. Then I ring Broadmoor to make sure and they say Ron hasn't been too well that day. Or I'll visit Ron and he'll say, 'I can feel that Reggie's a bit down and depressed at the moment – you must give him a ring.' Often I've had letters in the same post from both of them and both saying the same thing when there's no way they could have spoken to each other.

Physically, of course, the twins are identical. They dress differently – Reg in his jeans and Ron in his suits – but if they swapped clothes you wouldn't be able to tell which was which. They've both gone a bit grey since they were last photographed outside at their mother's funeral in 1982, but I think they've both become more distinguished-looking as they've got older and I think neither of them look their age.

They're a little touchy about their hearing. They've both gone a bit deaf over the years – although Ron is deaf in one ear and Reg is deaf in the other! This has led to a problem or two. The funniest involved Reg at Gartree. He and some of the other prisoners were having a shower. The showers are communal, but each man apparently has his own cubicle and there are no curtains between them so they were all washing and having a shouted conversation about music at the same time.

One man said he liked Annie Lennox and another was saying: Did you hear this on the radio? And then one of the other blokes said to Reg: 'Do you like Fleetwood Mac?'

Reg didn't reply.

'I said, "Do you like Fleetwood Mac?"' Next thing Reggie is in this man's shower cubicle scrubbing the bloke's back.

'Reg,' he said, 'what are you doing?'

'You said "Will you wash my back?"'

'No, I said, "Do you like Fleetwood Mac?"'

Poor old Reggie was terribly embarrassed and the next time I went to see him I couldn't resist teasing him. 'I heard about Fleetwood Mac,' I said.

He glared. 'What do you mean? That's not funny. I couldn't hear anything.'

That's another thing the twins have in common – their faces change in the same way when they think something isn't funny. They've both got a good sense of humour, especially Ron – but only so far. In fact Ron thought that story was hilarious.

The twins are always anxious for news of each other. One is always thinking of the other. There's been a lot of speculation about what Reg will do when he gets out, which should be in a couple of years with any luck, but I know where he'll be: up at Boadmoor.

Maybe he'll travel, and there are no doubt lots of things he'll want to catch up on, but he'd never do any business on his own and nothing would stop him being up at Broadmoor. He'll never be able to lead a normal life until Ron is out. It will always be the two of them.

Charlie is seven years older than Ron and Reg, and the twins also had a sister. Violet's first child was a girl, also called Violet, but sadly she died when she was just a baby. I have often wondered what the twins would have been like with a sister – a little protective, I think!

As life turned out, it's always been Charlie – and the twins, perhaps because of the age difference. Charlie would be the first to admit that. He was never deeply involved in the old Firm, although the police obviously thought differently. He went down for being an accessory to the murder of McVitie – and he was in bed asleep at the time!

I think I now understand, as well as anyone can, the relationship between Ron and Reg, but it was all a bit of a mystery in those early days. Every time Reg wrote to me and every time I saw him he'd ask me to visit Ron: 'Please go and see Ron' – and every time I'd say no. 'Ron wants to meet you,' he'd say, but I didn't want to go.

Reggie and I had become good friends. He wrote letters to me, we spoke on the phone, he even wrote a poem to me. He called it 'Whispering Dream'.

My whispering dream
As fresh as the morning dew
Smiling eyes oh so blue
Whispering dream I met out of the blue
It's a dream come true
She has it all
Physically she is great
She is my mate
Mentally she stimulates me
Oh how she excites me
Through and through
We blend together and entwine
It's good to know she is mine
She is like an angel
Without wings – My heart sings
Her beauty is ecstasy
Together we love till the sunset
She is the world to me
And has been since the day we met
That's the reason I named her
'Whispering Dream'
Because it's a dream come true!

I was very touched by the poem, although it wasn't strictly accurate. There was nothing romantic between Reggie and me. I think he only put 'she is mine' because it rhymed with 'entwine'! The truest line was: 'She is my mate.' I was. I still am. And, as a mate, Reggie wanted me to visit Ron.

To be honest, I was frightened to meet Ron. With all the things I'd heard about him I thought he was probably a raving lunatic, and I'd conjured up this picture in my mind of a real nut, sitting there with his glasses on upside down and saying horrible, fearsome things.

And then there was the place – Broadmoor. A hospital for the criminally insane. Just those words were enough to give me the creeps. I didn't want to go to see this man or this place. But I was Reggie's mate, so in the end, after a year of nagging and very reluctantly, I agreed to go.

It was a bit like knowing you've got a horrible hospital appointment. You don't want to go, but you know you must and somehow your feet take you there.

It was a crisp autumn day. The countryside around Broadmoor is quite beautiful, and as I drove up the tree-lined avenue to the hospital the leaves were turning. But my first sight of the place didn't do much to steady my nerves.

First you see the big gates then, up the hill, a huge Victorian building of orange brick. The Princess of Wales opened a new modern wing at the hospital in 1990, but what you see first is the old part which was built in 1870, when they called the place a lunatic asylum. And that's just what it looks like with rows of tiny cell windows all fitted with heavy bars.

The security at Broadmoor is probably the tightest anywhere in Britain – well, I suppose it does house the most dangerous people in the country – and you're very aware of it from the moment you arrive. The walls are all bomb-proof, there are security cameras everywhere. There's no way anyone could escape from Broadmoor. Once you're in, there's no getting out until they say so.

I joined the other visitors and we queued up to sign the big visitors' book. The man behind the glass screen asks who you want to see and then you have to write your name and address and your relationship to the patient while they phone over to the ward to tell the other screws to bring the patient down to the visitors' hall.

I wrote my name carefully and for relationship I put 'friend'. Once we'd all signed, the man came out and unlocked the big wrought-iron gates – and then locked them behind us.

He walked us across a courtyard to another gate and unlocked that one, ferried us through and locked it behind us. You're going deeper into Broadmoor now and as you walk along the corridors inside the building the screws are speaking into their walkie-talkies, warning the officer ahead of your approach.

You are monitored all the time and I have to admit I was very wary. The walls in this old part of the building were painted in that strange cream and green, and there was that indefinable smell – something between boiled cabbage and disinfectant.

But what I noticed most of all was the quiet. There is an incredible atmosphere of calm in the place, calm and peace. No one spoke as we walked along the corridors and through the sets of doors until we arrived at a room which looked like a school assembly hall, with a raised platform, a piano in the corner and lots of Formica-topped tables and chairs.

They headcounted us into the hall; they always do and they will never allow the visitors and the patients to move at the same time. The patients are moved in one at a time and you have to wait until they're seated at a table before you can join them. Or vice versa: you sit down first and the patients are escorted to you. You can't both arrive or leave at the same time. Necessary, I suppose, but horrible.

I looked around the hall at the men sitting at their tables, trying to keep a smile on my face and trying not to look too nervous. There was Ron. I knew it was him, of course, because he looked just like Reggie – but then I thought, that can't be him. He looks just like my bank manager! He was wearing a beautifully-cut navy-blue pin-striped suit, a crisp white shirt with double cuffs, silk tie and crocodile shoes. His hair was slicked back and at his wrists he wore a pair of gold cufflinks and on his little finger a gold pinkie ring. As I walked towards him he stood up, gave me a kiss on the cheek, and holding the chair out for me, said: 'Come and sit down next to me.'

'I've heard a lot about you from Reggie,' he said and I couldn't get over how softly-spoken he was, how polite and how gentle. This wasn't the nutcase I'd expected at all.

I told him I'd brought him some letters and some food but I'd had to put them into the special box for things the visitors bring – you're not allowed to give them straight to the patient.

He nodded and thanked me. 'Got any news?'

I told him I'd spoken to Reg. He was looking at me carefully. Ron always sits right up close to you and he never raises his voice.

His finger stroked my cheek. 'Look at your skin, aren't you young, look at your lovely teeth . . .'

I just kept looking at him and listening to this lovely soft voice. The other patients and their visitors were just feet away, but I didn't see anyone else in the hall at all. Ron has this thing about him, it's a kind of aura; you don't want to look anywhere else. He's got soft brown eyes, like Reggie's, and they hold you.

Everyone says the same thing when they meet Ron. They don't expect him to be so gentle, so they're surprised. And they're drawn to him. He's got charisma; that's the word.

'Got any news?' he said again.

So I told him all the news and we were chatting about everything and anything. I couldn't get over how nice he was. Then another man arrived to visit him – a big man in a big suit.

'No, don't go,' said Ron, and introduced me to his friend. Joey Pyle. They had things to talk about and I tried to sit back out of the way, but Ron kept saying: 'No, come over here . . .'

The time passed so quickly I couldn't believe I'd been there for two hours and it was time to go. Usually Ron leaves before the end of visiting time. He doesn't like going with the others because he doesn't like being herded around and also too many people want to chat to him and ask him questions on the way back.

But this time he waited until they called the name of his

ward, Somerset, where the Yorkshire Ripper was also a patient at the time.

Ron stood up and put my coat around my shoulders. 'Thank you for coming. I'd like to see you again. Would you come up again?' he said.

'Of course I will,' I said.

Joey and I had to stand and wait while the patients left – so we watched him disappear down the corridor. Ron turned and waved and as a joke Joey put his arms around me and winked: 'See you, Ron!'

Ron laughed. It was only later, on my wedding day, that one of the screws said to me: 'You remember that first visit, Kate? When I was walking back with Ron to his ward Ron turned to me and said: "See that girl, I'm going to marry that girl!"'

Marriage was the last thing on my mind as I walked out of Broadmoor that first time. But I was in shock. He was different to what I expected, so different to any other man I'd ever met.

I said goodbye to Joey and I went my way and he went his. As I drove down the motorway I couldn't stop thinking about Ron. It was ridiculous. I kept telling myself it was ridiculous. It wasn't that I fancied him, it wasn't that. There was just something about him, something between us.

I didn't want to leave him there; he was so nice, I wanted to take him home with me. I went straight back to Harry's.

'Harry, he's lovely, he's really lovely.' Harry just smiled – Harry often knows things about me before I even know them myself!

Two days later, I was looking out of the window when I saw what looked like a big bunch of flowers on legs coming up the path. The bouquet was so big you could hardly see the delivery man!

It didn't register at first. 'Blimey,' I thought, 'who's that from?'

The card said: 'Love from Ron.'

Harry laughed. 'You're playing a very dangerous game here,' he said. 'One of them's going to fall for you. You know that, don't you?'

'Rubbish,' I said. But a few days later a parcel arrived – a beautiful gold chain. And a card: 'Love from Ron.' That night the phone rang. It was Wilf Pine, an old friend of Ron's. 'The Colonel wants to see you again,' he said in a gruff voice.

As soon as I heard from Wilf I knew I wanted to go and see Ron again as soon as possible. If I'm honest, maybe I'd been waiting for the call. I knew Ron couldn't phone me and I couldn't call him – in those days they were only allowed one phone call a year and that was three whole months away, on Christmas Day.

I wanted to see him again. I couldn't get him out of my mind, how calm and gentle he was. When I saw Reggie he ran circles round me, but Ron was different. He was almost humble in a strange way – I didn't expect that. It was confusing.

I suppose, yes, I was slightly in awe of him and I'd never felt that with Reggie. But it was more than that. He has a presence and everyone feels it, even the screws. They treat him with respect and he seldom gives them any trouble. Everyone likes Ron.

The next time I drove up to Broadmoor, I didn't feel as nervous in one way but I was more nervous in another. The place didn't hold the same fear for me. The staff there are really very kind and very helpful, and there is nothing menacing about the atmosphere, even if the building is a bit formidable.

This time I was more nervous about seeing Ron, nervous and excited all at the same time. I had a feeling that this meeting was going to be important for me in some way, although I didn't know how. It was a premonition. He was already there, waiting for me in the hall when I arrived, just as he had been the first time. He saw me, stood up and shook my hand and gave me a kiss on the cheek. We sat down next to each other.

I smiled at him.

'Right,' he said. 'If I've got something to say I don't beat around the bush, Kate. If you don't marry Reggie, will you marry me?'

I'd maybe expected him to say something, but not this! I looked at him, shocked, and then I just laughed. I mean the whole thing was ridiculous.

'I'm not going to marry Reggie. I'm just friends with Reggie, that's all. I mean, I've never even thought of anything else.' And that was the truth. I liked Reggie. We were friends who liked a good laugh together, but Reggie had never shown any desire for it to be anything more than that. Me neither.

'Well, will you marry me then?' said Ron.

I didn't know what to say, so I just made a joke of the whole thing and we didn't mention it again for the rest of the visit. As I got up to leave, he helped me on with my coat as usual, shook my hand and kissed me on the cheek.

'I'll call you tonight if you like,' I said. 'After "Coronation Street", at eight o'clock.'

'Yes, all right.'

'I'll phone you every night at eight if you like.' Strangely, it seemed the most natural thing to say.

'Yeah, all right.'

I knew I wouldn't be able to speak to him, but at least I could say: 'Tell Ron I rang and tell him goodnight.' It was only much later that I found out that that was what the twins' mum used to do. Violet would ring Broadmoor after 'Coronation Street' at eight and say the same thing. Strange. Ron's always saying how much I'm like his mum, always laughing, the way I kid people and joke. I don't know. I would very much like to have met her.

That day, driving back, I still couldn't quite believe what he'd said, although something in me wasn't too surprised. I think I knew from the first moment I met him that we were meant to be something special to each other. Don't ask me how – I just knew.

But I still felt numb. I went back to Harry's and said: 'You'll never guess what? He's only asked me to marry him!' Harry didn't look surprised in the slightest!

I kept running over the conversation in my mind. I didn't know what was going to happen, but I did know after that what the score was where Ron was concerned and how his mind was working. Later, I realized it was the first and only time that the first thing he said to me was something other than: 'Got any news?'

After that I started seeing Ron three times a week. The journey up there and back was a drag, but it was worth it, and it was soon obvious that other people knew what Ron had in mind too. I began to hear from his friends. If they wanted to know which would be the best day to visit him Ron would say, 'Ask Kate', or if they wanted to get a message to Ron he'd say, 'Tell Kate'.

Or sometimes his friends would just ring and say: 'I saw the Colonel today and he told me to phone and say hello.' More people and business acquaintances of Ron and Reg's get to see Ron because he's allowed visits during the week and four at weekends. Reggie, being in prison, is only allowed two visits a month.

Soon it got to a stage where the phone never stopped ringing, and I'd take all sorts of messages for Ron. I always say that Ron and Reg are like spiders. They've got their web around them, and in that web are loads of people and, as you get closer and closer to them, the deeper you're drawn into the web and the more things you get to do for them.

But I wasn't complaining. The more Ron and I met and talked the better I liked him. He's not a soppy man; we don't go in for that gooey stuff, thank goodness. I wouldn't like it if he were that type of man. I don't like soppy men.

But I know he cares. I just have to look at him and he looks at me and there's a certain look that passes between us and we both know. He courted me in a lovely, gentle, old-fashioned way. He was always sending me flowers, still is. He isn't much of a one for writing, but I've kept all the cards that arrived with his flowers. And there have been times when I've thrown a wobbly and said: 'You don't care about me.' You know, the usual way that

ıe chefs at Broadmoor really did us proud with the wedding
ke – two hearts, iced in pink and white. I loved the cake – and
ıthed the curtains ! We kept them drawn so we couldn't see
e bars at the windows.

*Above:* Me with Santa. I can't remember what he was promising me for Christmas but I obviously wasn't impressed!

*Opposite top left and right:* Aren't they sweet?! That's Ronnie or the left and Reggie, right, both a few months old. The twins are identical and Reggie is the eldest by ten minutes.

*Opposite below:* More than thirty years later and the twins no longer look quite so sweet! Even so, I think Ron, on the left, looks very handsome !

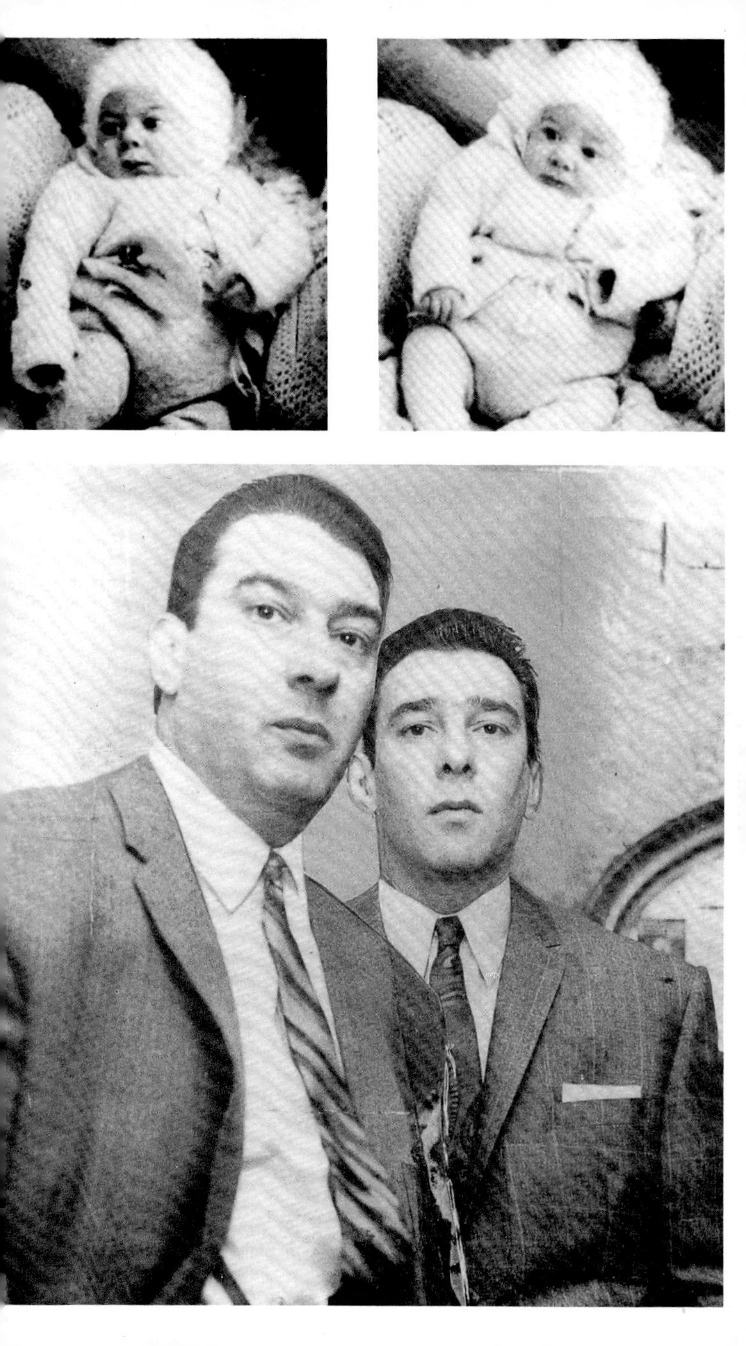

*Top:* Ron, on the left, and Reg at school.

*Above:* They weren't exactly model pupils but they both loved boxing from an early age – and they both had a good left hook even then! This was taken in 1946.

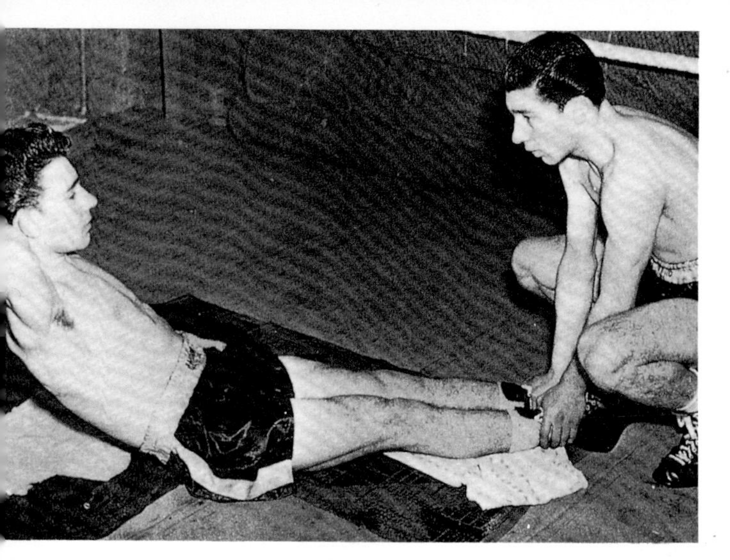

*ɔ:* Six years later, in 1952, the twins' boxing career was
;inning to get them noticed. Reggie, on the left, was London
ıools' Champion and unbeaten as an amateur.

*ɔve:* Another wedding day. Ronnie, on the left, with Reggie
ł his bride, Frances.

*Top:* Ronnie with Lord Boothby, on the left, and Leslie Holt. Holt tried to blackmail Lord Boothby over his alleged affair wi Ron. Holt later died in hospital where he'd gone for an operation on his warts.

*Above:* Ron has always loved animals. He and Reggie bought their Mum, Violet, a racehorse. Unfortunately it was no Derby winner!

eggie, on the left, and Ronnie leaving Ronnie's London flat in
edra Court. The twins have always been snappy dressers!

*Top:* Ronnie has always loved dogs. Here he is with his English Bull terrier, Mr. Bill.

*Above:* Ronnie used to enjoy travelling and he and Reggie loved visiting North Africa. Here's Ron having a drink with friends at an outside cafe in Morocco.

women carry on every now and then! He'll never say anything at the time, but next day the flowers arrive and there's a simple note: 'I do care – Ron.'

I discovered that he's the most generous person in the world – he's always giving things away. Drives me mad sometimes. I'd buy him a suit or a shirt and then I'd say, 'Where's that suit? Where's that shirt?' 'Oh,' he'd say. 'So and so is feeling a bit down and he said he liked it, so I gave it to him!'

Another thing struck me after seeing Ron a few times: he never moans, especially about the time he's served. That surprised me too. When you think of some criminals and the awful things they've done – far worse than Ron – and now they've done their time and are living a normal life outside and there's Ron after twenty-five years... Well, I expected him to go on about it. But all he ever says is: 'There's no point in moaning, there's people worse off than me.' That is typical of Ron.

He's also very kind and we have a good laugh together. He's got a lovely dry sense of humour. Sometimes on those visits I'd do nutty things just to make him laugh or shock him. Having been inside for so long there's so many things he doesn't know about, little things, things we take for granted. Can you imagine what it's like never to be able to turn your own light on or off? In Broadmoor and high-security prisons they go off automatically at night. Reggie told me that when he stopped being a Category A prisoner after seventeen years and was transferred to a cell where you were actually allowed to control your lights he spent one evening just turning them on and off. It was such a novelty.

Sometimes I talk to Ron about Taffy, my dog, and he says: 'How nice to be able to stroke a dog. I'd love that. I'd love to own a dog again.'

And we joke that when he finally gets out he's going to find it very difficult to go in and out of doors – he'll just stand in front of one and expect it to open for him!

In top-security prisons and hospitals doors are opened for you, or automatically, so Ron hasn't opened a door for himself in twenty-five years!

When we were finally allowed to speak together on the phone every day, I brought him in some phone cards and he said: 'And what the hell are they?'

He said the same when I told him about my kissagram business: 'Kissagrams – what on earth are they?'

And one day I really managed to shock him. At the time I wore false nails, but Ron didn't know that. 'Haven't you got pretty nails?' he said to me during one visit.

'Oh Ron,' I said. 'You think you're really tough, don't you? Well, look at this!' And I dramatically pulled off one of my fingernails. Poor old Ron went: 'Aaargh!'

My visits fell into a kind of routine. I got to know him and the more I knew him the better I liked him. We weren't awkward with each other – I felt I could tell him anything and I did. I got to know the staff, too, and they were always friendly. We'd have a chat and then I'd meet Ron. 'Got any news?' And he'd talk business for a while and then we'd just chat and every now and then he'd say: 'Well, are you going to marry me then?'

And I kept saying: 'Oh, I don't know . . .' and I'd grin at him. Then one day I said, 'I'll only marry you when you tell me you love me.' Ron hates all that sort of sentimental stuff, so he wouldn't.

It became a running joke between us. I kept teasing him. When he phoned me I knew that there were usually people listening in, so I'd cry dramatically down the phone: 'Ron! Ron! Tell me you love me! Tell me, Ron!' And he'd say 'Stop it! Leave it out! People are listening – they can hear you!' and I'd hear one of the screws practically choking with laughter.

Then one day Wilf Pine rang me. He sounded a bit embarrassed. 'Er, I saw the Colonel today and he told me to tell you he loves you. He told me to tell you that. He said you know what he means.'

Poor Wilf. I don't know what he made of it all.

I just laughed. 'Yes,' I said. 'I know what he means.'

The next day I drove up to see Ron.

'You got my message, then?' he said.

'Yes,' I said. 'But don't think I'm going to make it easy for you! Do you love me?'

Ron kind of sighed the way men do. 'I suppose I do. Now are we going to get married or what?'

I didn't say a word.

'Well, all right, I do love you, Kate,' he said quietly. 'In my own way I do love you.'

'Well, let's get married then!' And I gave him a kiss.

We spent the rest of the visit talking about the wedding. At least I did. 'Got any news?' said Ron, the proposal safely out of the way.

The family were really pleased when they heard we were engaged. Wilf introduced me to Ron's brother,

Charlie, for the first time in a pub and he was really friendly.

'Congratulations,' he said, 'I've heard a lot about you from Ron and Reg.'

Reggie wrote me a nice letter. 'Congratulations to you and the Colonel on the wedding. He's a good-looking chap! Ha, ha!'

Ron and I were feeling pretty pleased too, but on one visit Ron sat close to me and said: 'You know it could be difficult for you now,' he said. 'When it gets out and into the press that we're getting married you'll have a lot to cope with for a while. It won't be easy, Kate. You don't know what you're letting yourself in for.'

'Oh, don't be daft,' I said. 'Of course I do. Everything will be all right. Don't worry. I'll cope.'

And I really did think I would cope. I knew I was doing the right thing. I loved Ron and he loved me, in our own way. I wanted to marry Ron, he wanted to marry me. What could be simpler? I wish now I'd listened more closely to what Ron was saying then maybe I would have been more prepared for all that happened. Maybe I would have coped better.

As usual Ron was right. I didn't really know what I was letting myself in for.

## CHAPTER FOUR

# *Trouble and Strife*

One man tried to spoil it. One man tried to spoil what for Ron and I was to be one of the most special days of our lives: our wedding day.

At least, we feel he tried to spoil it. Reggie wasn't there. And Reggie wasn't there because of one man: Peter Gillett.

Even now I find it hard to write his name. To me he will always be Slag Gillett. Or just Slag for short.

Ron never liked him. Reggie thought he was a good friend. In my opinion Reggie was mistaken. And Reggie and Gillett are no longer friends.

It's not a nice story. But probably the most ironic part of it is that it was Ron and Reg who saved this man's life. If it wasn't for them Gillett could have been found floating up somewhere long ago.

Gillett, who's now thirty-three, met Reggie when they were both in Parkhurst prison and they became close friends.

Reggie likes the company of young people. He and Gillett both used the gym to keep fit and Reggie thought Gillett showed great talent as a singer. He went out of his way to help him – he wrote a song for him to record when he came out and, more than that, he even contacted his old friend Jools Holland to ask him to help Gillett to get a recording contract.

Gillett was released in the late 1980s and, in part thanks to Reg, managed to make the beginnings of a career in show-business. Thanks to Reg he got a small part in the film *The Krays*.

Thanks to Reg he received a lot of publicity as he talked of his friendship with one of the famous Krays. There were headlines in the papers such as the one in the *Independent*: 'REGGIE KRAY'S GOING TO MAKE HIM A STAR.' In 1989 Gillett appeared on TV's 'Treasure Hunt' programme for Channel 4 with lovely Annabel Croft, a nice girl who before going into showbusiness used to be Britain's most promising woman tennis player.

For the show Annabel, Gillett and two others were 'marooned' on a tropical island off Sri Lanka and the idea was that they had to survive for a week.

The show resulted in huge headlines. The newspapers alleged that Annabel was furious because Gillett had sexually harassed her on the island. Gillett denied it in the press – at length. But he did admit that Annabel had hit him where it hurts most.

That was early in 1989 – the year of my wedding. I didn't take much notice of the story. I knew Gillett because I'd delivered some papers to him from Reggie every now and then. I was friendly but no more than that. I thought Gillett fancied himself. Later a woman detective was quoted in the newspapers as saying that he was so obsessed about his looks that 'if he were a chocolate he'd eat himself!'

When we met it was: 'Hello, how are you?' A peck on the cheek maybe, perhaps a quick chat, but only out of politeness. Nothing more. As Ron says: 'Good manners cost nothing.' To me he was just another of the twins' many friends who I met because of Reg.

So I read the story about Annabel Croft and thought little of it. With hindsight, perhaps it was an omen.

I'm not daft. But I have to admit that four short years ago I was very green. When I agreed to marry Ron I knew I was not marrying an ordinary man. I knew I would be married to the Krays and the whole kit and caboodle that goes with them, including the legends, the lies and the mystery that has always surrounded them.

Even so, it didn't sink in that marrying Ron made me a target, too.

So many people have made money out of writing about the Krays. Some of the words have been true, fair and accurate. Some have been . . . well, depends on your point of view! And a lot that has been written about them is totally false, and absolute rubbish.

The pressure started building up as soon as people found out we were getting married. Ron warned me, but I took no notice. I should have listened. He's had it for most of his life – people saying things, making up stories. I never even thought of it – why should people make up stories about me, why should they say horrible things? Believe me, I've learned my lesson since.

As soon as one of the Broadmoor nurses had leaked it to the press that Ron and I were getting married the phone didn't stop ringing. 'Is it true you're going to marry Ronnie Kray?' I didn't know what to do so I kept saying, 'No comment, no comment', then I asked Ron what to do.

Ron said the best thing to do would be to go with one paper. 'Give them an exclusive,' he said, 'and they'll pay you a bit of money and the others will leave you alone.' So that's what I did and, true enough, they did pay me a bit of money and the rest of the journalists went away for a while and that, I thought, was that.

I was running around like a loony preparing for the wedding. I'd given up doing kissagrams myself because Ron had warned me I might be set up. But one day someone rang and booked a topless kissagram for a party in Wrotham in Kent. Harry took the booking and they asked for me by name. But there was nothing unusual in that. I had quite a few regulars who'd ring and ask for me if they were having a party.

I nearly didn't do the job, I was so knackered, but there was no one else. Our other girl who worked for us was off sick. I was also skint so I thought, 'Ten minutes' work – forty-five pounds' and off we went that night to the hotel, me in my schoolgirl's uniform and underneath my topless basque, stockings and suspenders.

As usual, Harry drove and we turned up on time at this flashy hotel. They said they didn't want me to do the kissagram in the bar. The place was really posh and I suppose they were worried it might offend some of the customers, so the party was being held in a function room.

And there was Birthday Boy, whoever he was, an accountant I was told, and about twelve guests. I did my bit, took off my uniform, sang my little song and they took pictures of me. Nothing unusual about that – they always take pictures at these birthday parties.

Then one of these blokes said: 'Would you whip him?' So I said OK. Nothing unusual about that either – you'd be amazed the number of times I'm asked to whip the

Birthday Boy – usually one 'lash' for every year! I made him bend over a 'desk' and take his shirt off and then I gently walloped him with someone's belt. All pretend, of course, and everyone was having a good laugh and a joke.

It was all normal stuff. In fact, when you're a topless kissagram girl you don't get mauled about. The men think they're being really daring just having you there at all. Most of them are scared to death – especially Birthday Boy, who's usually bright-red with embarrassment and terrified of what's going to happen next. It's all good clean fun.

So that was that. A nice crowd they were, too. They even gave me twenty quid tip – brilliant! And off I went home with Harry to put my feet up and watch the telly.

Later that night, someone from the papers rang and said they had a story that I'd had an affair with Gillett.

I said: 'What? I don't know what you're talking about.'

'Have you got any comment?'

'About what? I don't know what you're talking about.'

Next day I open the paper and there's a story about me! It alleged that I'd had sex with Gillett dressed in my schoolgirl kissagram outfit in the back of a BMW at a local golf course. The story didn't quote Gillett, but an unnamed 'informant'. If that wasn't bad enough, there was a picture of me – doing the kissagram at that party, me topless and 'whipping' a man bending over a table!

I couldn't believe it. The story was totally untrue. As I've said, I knew Gillett but what were they talking about? I had no idea who the informant was, but whoever it was was a real bastard! And, as for the picture, I'd been set up just as Ron had warned me I would be. That was no birthday party, that was no accountant, it was a crowd of journalists.

I was really upset. I burst into tears and I couldn't stop crying. The phone rang and it was Broadmoor – Ron couldn't ring out at that time. They said: 'Ron's really upset and wants to know if you're all right. Ron says you must come up and see him.'

I said no. It wasn't that I didn't want to see Ron. He was the one person I did want to see. But all those other people. All I wanted to do was hide. I couldn't go to Broadmoor. I knew Ron didn't believe a word of it – he knew Gillett and he's never liked him. Everyone Ron knows is of the opinion that he's a slag. It was the other people I couldn't face.

Broadmoor rang back. 'Ron's really insistent,' they said. 'You've got to come.'

'I can't,' I said. 'I can't face anyone.'

They kept saying: 'Calm down, calm down,' and I kept crying and saying, 'I can't, I can't.'

But in the end I wanted to see Ron, so Harry drove me. I looked terrible, big puffy eyes, big fat nose and my face all red. I waited outside until everyone had gone in so it looked like I was late and then I went into the big hall. Ron was waiting for me.

I felt as though everybody froze. They sort of stopped and they were all looking at me. But as soon as I walked in Ron stood up and said: 'Kate' and he put his arms around me and made a fuss of me. I'll never forget how Ron did that. He was showing everyone that he knew the story was rubbish and that he was supporting me.

Ron was brilliant. I started to cry, but Ron would have none of it. He didn't want me crying in front of all those people. And, anyway, what did I have to cry about? I'd done nothing wrong. He knew that. He told me not to worry, he'd sort it out. He tried to cheer me up. But he was upset, too, I could tell. Most of all he was angry. I'd never seen him so angry.

'Dirty slag,' he said. Ron had never had time for the slag anyway. He might have been a friend of Reggie's, but Ron never liked him and he knew as soon as he saw him what he was like. Ron's very astute like that about people.

It was a terrible time. It would have been bad enough if it had stopped there, but it didn't. Things went from bad to worse.

As I was driving down the motorway Reggie rang me on my mobile phone. I was crying and Reggie was mad too. But this was his friend and he trusted him and he said: 'If he says that's what happened, it did.'

'But it didn't,' I said. 'It didn't.'

It was no good. Ron believed me. Reggie didn't. In a way I understood that. You see, the twins are so loyal. They are loyal and they expect their friends to be the same. It is always hard for either of them to accept that other people don't have the same standards of loyalty that they do.

The next day the papers picked up on the story again. There was a story about how I'd shamed the Kray brothers. My God! I'd never do that. Never! I was about to become a Kray myself. I felt terrible, as if I'd let Ron down.

Everywhere I went I felt ashamed, although I had

absolutely nothing to be ashamed of. Even my mum thought badly of me. She told my brother that when she went to work at her paper factory the next day she felt really ashamed of me and she came home crying. It was embarrasssing for her – one minute I'm marrying Ronnie Kray and the next I'm a slag in the paper.

I'll never forgive that bastard. He upset me and my family, he upset Ron, but looking back perhaps the worst part was that it caused a bit of a rift for a while between Ron and Reg.

Ron argued with Reggie about it and so did I. I went up to see Reggie and we had a terrible row about it. And, in the end, that's why Reggie didn't come to the wedding, which was a great shame. Ron and I would both have liked him there. It wasn't the same without him.

Of course it wasn't long before the twins made up. Whatever happens, whatever it's about, they can never fight about anything for any length of time.

After the second day of stories, Ron decided that he'd had enough. He gave an interview to the *Sun* newspaper and, as a result of what Ron said, Gillett sued the paper. Ron was cross – an understatement! Things were getting out of hand. Gillett just wouldn't leave it alone. I had to see the *Sun*'s lawyers. They settled out of court. They published an apology, as they were legally bound to do.

Gillett insisted to Ron and Reg that he had never told the newspaper that I'd had sex with him anyway. He wasn't the 'informant', he said. But what Ron never told me was that Gillett had visited him in Broadmoor shortly after we'd told people we were getting married. And, while he was there, he made the same accusation. Ron never told me because he knew it would upset me. But apparently Ron was furious about it.

Someone else who was there at the time later told me: 'I've never seen Ron so angry. He didn't shout, he didn't threaten him in any way, he said very little. But a look of pure anger crossed his face. You could tell he was furious.'

The other thing I was told later was that Gillett had written to Reggie when he heard about me and Ron and said that Ron shouldn't get involved with a girl like me. Why? you ask. Because I was a . . . kissagram girl! Funny really, when you consider he's been inside.

I really don't know why Gillett had it in for me. He was a close friend of Reggie's and he knew I was friends with Reg. Then I met Ron and we were going to be married. I was going to be family. I was family. I really don't understand it.

Maybe he was jealous. Who knows?

Meanwhile, Ron was angry. He was also worried. Ron has many friends on the outside and all of them knew the story of what had happened. It was hardly surprising that they thought Gillett was taking a diabolical liberty. He was. But Ron didn't want anyone doing anything out of friendship on his behalf which could jeopardize his, or, more realistically, Reggie's chance of release.

Slowly news reached him that some people were so incensed by what Gillett was doing that they thought he should be taken care of. Gillett had gone into hiding for fear of his life after one man smacked him in the mouth and another took pot shots at him. We heard that his house was being guarded by plain-clothes policemen.

This was getting out of hand. The news on the street was that a hit was out on Gillett. Ron would have none of it. He did the only thing he could. He let it be known that he didn't want Gillett hurt.

He understood that his friends, and even people who didn't know him except by reputation, thought the man had taken a terrible liberty. He understood their loyalty to him and that, out of respect, they would want to sort the slag out. But he didn't want it. So Ron managed to get the word out that the slag was to be left in one piece.

So I honestly believe that Ron and Reg saved that man's life. Without them he might have been found dead by now. But they said no.

Even so, we heard he was seriously hurt. Someone took it upon themselves to do the bastard. I don't know how it happened, or where. I didn't ask details. I knew that Gillett could not go anywhere in London and I know that Ron didn't order it to happen. I also know that some people who admire the Krays take it upon themselves to correct what they see as wrong. I know that if Ron and Reg hadn't put a stop to it God knows what would have happened. I also have to admit I didn't cry buckets over what happened.

So much trouble, so many tears, so much grief and for what? Money. People making money out of Ron and Reg. As usual.

The police arrested Gillett in 1992. At Christmas, he went down for eight years for his involvement in a drugs deal. Reggie is more forgiving than me, more charitable. He suggested I let bygones be bygones and send him a note to wish him all the best and offer my condolences.

I told Reg: 'The only thing I'd send him is a bomb!'

'That's not very festive, Kate,' said Reggie.

'And I hope he gets gang-raped!' I said to Ron and he just laughed.

Gillett is now languishing in prison and what he did hasn't been forgotten. Just a few weeks ago someone rang me and said that Gillett had had a row with another prisoner.

Gillett apparently went out on the landing and started shouting his mouth off: 'You lot will be sorry when Reggie Kray finds out about this!'

The caller wanted to know 'Is Gillett all right with Reggie?' because otherwise he was going to be slashed.

It was a difficult question to answer. As I told him: 'I'm hardly the person to ask.'

I don't know the gory details – I don't want to know – but I do know Gillett was striped. I do know it wasn't the first time and I imagine it won't be the last – not with the mouth he's got on him. And, to be honest, I won't lose any sleep over it.

Gillett and Reggie are no longer friends. From Reggie's point of view that's sad, because it's horrible for him to have trusted and been fond of someone who lets you down so. But Gillett was stupid. Ron has always played fair and expects others to do the same. If they don't, I think it can sometimes turn into a learning experience.

CHAPTER FIVE

# *Cracking Up*

'You've got to go to the police now, Kate. Not later. Not tomorrow. Now.' I couldn't believe what I was hearing. This was Reggie talking and with Reggie and Ron you sort out a problem yourself. The last thing you do is go to the police, but Reggie was serious. There's nothing he or Ron could have done from the inside and Reggie didn't like the sound of it.

And as it turned out, Reggie was right. Thank God I did as he said.

I went down to the local police station and went up to reception.

'Look, this is really difficult for me. But I've got to tell you. I've been having these crank phonecalls...'

'Name?'

'Well,' I said, 'that's the difficulty. It's Kray, Kate Kray. I'm Ron's wife.'

They took me into a little room and introduced me to a CID woman called Pat Geary. A really nice lady and very understanding.

'I don't want to make a fuss,' I said. 'But I want these calls to stop.'

And I did. I don't scare easily, but I was beginning to get scared.

It was so silly, really. It had all started when Ron and I had a bit of a ruck. I can't even remember what it was about. Nothing important, probably something I'd forgotten to do for him. I was in a foul mood, a real temper. I threw my wedding ring on the table and stomped off. It landed in the ashtray.

Ron rummaged through the ashtray, found the ring and dusted it off. Then he went up to another lady who was visiting and said: 'Here, you might like this.'

That's typical Ron. Unless I'm careful he'd give everything away.

But this was a nice lady. She knew what Ron was like, how generous he is, and she could also see that we'd had a tiff, so she got my number and phoned me. 'I've got your ring,' she said. 'I'll send it back to you.' I was really grateful. I'd only thrown it away it in the heat of the moment.

I gave her my address and she sent it registered post. After that I often talked to her when she was up at Broadmoor to see a friend of her husband's. He, the husband, had been in Broadmoor for eighteen years before they let him out. I didn't know what he'd done – you never know what they're in for and I don't usually ask.

He was a little man, about sixty-five, and he wore a wig. I thought he was a bit weird and I didn't take much notice of him. But I got quite friendly with his wife. We'd meet in the ladies' when I was doing my hair and things. She was very nice. I didn't see her for a while, then one day I was up there seeing Ron and there she was. She'd come back again with her husband to visit this friend of his. That's quite unusual. Once you've left Broadmoor you have to have special permission to go back and see anyone.

'How's it going?' I said. She'd stuck by her husband all the time he was in Broadmoor, but I realized that however pleased she was to have him home it must have been hard for them both to readjust after all that time.

'It's terrible, Kate,' she said. 'It's sex. He's sex-mad. He wants it morning, noon and night. I don't think I can cope with it.'

I looked at her. She was upset.

'It's terrible. He wakes me up in the night all the time. And during the day . . . if I'm just unpacking the shopping into the fridge he wants it. I'm trying to eat my dinner and he wants it, I'm doing the ironing, he wants it . . . I just don't know what to do . . .'

Poor woman. I felt sorry for her. But after that I didn't think much more about it. I was glad she'd sent back my ring, but it wasn't really my problem.

Months went by, then one day the phone rang and the voice said: 'It's Steve.'

It took me a moment to remember who he was.

'Oh yeah, how are you doing?'

'She's left me.'

'Oh, I'm sorry to hear that, Steve.'

'It's all because of sex . . .'

'Oh . . .'

'Perhaps with Ron inside I could be his stand-in with you . . .' And then he started saying all these disgusting things. Horrible things.

I said: 'I don't think so, I don't think you ought to be talking to me like this, Steve, do you? Just stop it. Let's forget about it. 'Bye.'

I put the phone down feeling a bit sick. Ron's stand-in?

The bloke was mad! How did he get my number? From his wife. Well, he's tried phoning once, he won't try it again, I thought.

Wrong. The calls kept coming and the things he said turned my stomach. I tried to keep calm about it. 'Look,' I said, 'if you keep ringing me like this I'm going to have to tell Ron about it.'

But he kept on and on. In the end I was almost afraid to pick up the phone. If I did and it was him I'd shout: 'Don't phone me any more!' And hang up.

I didn't want to tell Ron. I knew he'd be angry, but in the end it got so bad I had to. I just told him the truth. 'He keeps ringing and saying these filthy things and that he wants to be your stand-in.'

Ron was livid. It was a liberty, he said. He'd sort it out. And he did. He wrote to the wife, saying: 'Your husband keeps pestering Kate and tell him to leave it out.'

The next thing I know, I get a phonecall from the wife. 'We've heard from Ron,' she said. 'He says Steve has been pestering you and it's got to stop, but I can't believe it. Of course he hasn't been phoning you.'

'I'm sorry, but he has. I haven't made this up. Why should I? I don't want any fuss – I just want it to stop.'

I felt sorry for her, being married to a bastard like that.

After that the calls stopped and I was very relieved. Unless you've been through it yourself you've no idea how horrible it is to dread the phone ringing and how you jump every time it does.

After a while I forgot about it. Then, on Christmas Eve, the phone rang again. It was him and this time he sounded really mad. 'You fucking bitch, I'm coming to kill you.'

I don't want to tell you all the details of what he said he'd do to me – he wanted to stick knives into me, and there was more. It makes me sick just to think about it.

For the next three days, all over Christmas, he didn't stop ringing.

As soon as I hung up, the phone rang again and it was Reggie. He could tell immediately that I was upset and when I told him what was happening he told me to go to the police straight away.

The police were very kind. They told me to go home, ring Broadmoor and tell them what was happening and said they'd be in touch. I rang Broadmoor and they were very concerned. They told me I was right to go to the police, but I still felt uneasy about it. I didn't like making this fuss. But Reggie was right. As soon as I put the phone down it was the CID. They'd been on to Broadmoor too.

'Stay there, Kate. Wait until we get there. We're coming straight round. You're not alone, are you? Is someone there with you?'

Yes, thank God, Harry was with me.

When the police arrived the news wasn't good. Steve lived up north, and after leaving Broadmoor he still had to check in with the local police but he seemed to have disappeared.

'We've made inquiries,' the CID man said. 'He's extremely dangerous. We want to move you to a safe house. There'll be someone with you all the time. We'll put pressure pads under the carpet here so we'll get the alarm if he turns up.'

But I didn't want to go. Harry said: 'Don't worry about her. I'll stick with her all the time. I'll take care of her.'

To be honest I felt safer with Harry – and what the police didn't know was he'd already gone and borrowed a shotgun from a local scrap dealer. Even so, it was worrying. The man was on his way to kill me – that was obvious from what he'd said on the phone . . . He really wanted to do all those things to me.

The police weren't happy about me staying with Harry, but I insisted. The next couple of days were worrying. Every time the phone rang I jumped. Sometimes it was him. He was getting nearer, he said. The police were worried. He was a complete nut-case, they said. We can't find him. Get her out of the house. But I felt safest with Harry.

I suppose it's an understatement to say it spoiled Christmas. I spent the holiday with Harry and saw my family and we tried to put it to the back of our minds when we were doing all the usual things, eating and drinking and opening presents. But you couldn't forget that he was out there somewhere.

Every now and then the police turned up to see if I was OK. Once the CID lady, Pat, was there and the phone rang. She answered it.

'You fucking bitch,' said the voice. 'I'm going to kill you.'

She was very cool. 'Is that you, Steve?'

'I'm going to fucking kill you.'

She tried to keep him on the phone. I didn't like the look of it. Why couldn't they catch him? She left and told me to try and keep calm. Would I reconsider and go to a safe house? No. I'd stay with Harry. The next day they picked him up. I don't know how – I think they must have finally managed to trace the calls. But what frightened me was that he'd made the journey from north to south and when they finally grabbed him he was in Maidstone, only two miles from my home.

He had got very close.

The CID woman rang me immediately. 'Don't worry. We've got him.' And then she told me just how worried they'd been. They knew why he'd been sent down in the first place and it wasn't a pleasant story. Years ago, he'd done to a young girl exactly what he was threatening to do to me.

'We didn't tell you at the time. We didn't want to make it worse for you.'

I didn't want to press charges. The idea of me sending someone back to prison just seemed so wrong. But the policewoman talked a lot of sense.

'OK,' she said. 'Suppose you don't press charges. And a few months go by and then you read in the papers that he's done all those things to another girl, maybe a young girl. And you know that you could have stopped that. How are you going to feel?'

She was right – I wouldn't have been able to live with myself. I went and saw Ron. He knew what was going on and he was worried about me – he was also furious.

'Ron, I don't want to press charges but she says...'

'Well, you've got to press charges because she's right. You'd never be able to live with yourself. He should be locked up. He's a nonce.'

So I did press charges. The court allowed him out on bail, even though the police opposed it, as long as he reported to his local police station three times a day and didn't come anywhere near Maidstone – or me. In fact I think he probably wouldn't have dared. There were and still are people who would probably take care of him if he did.

But for reasons I can't go into now, legal reasons, when it finally came to court I told them that I would agree to him being conditionally discharged as long as he didn't come anywhere near me. I don't know what's happened to him since and I don't want to know.

For me, that episode marred the beginning of my marriage to Ronnie. Ron was very concerned for me.

I was determined to make our marriage work and one loony wasn't going to make me run to the divorce courts, although I now knew that being a Kray made me a target for people other than the press.

I knew, too, full well that people said our marriage would never last.

Someone told me that Kelvin MacKenzie, the Editor of the *Sun* newspaper, even had money on it. I was told he bet someone two grand that it would all be over in a year. I'm happy to say that at the end of that year some charity apparently did quite well out of him.

In November 1993 Ron and I will have been married for four years.

To be honest, it's been touch and go at times. Ron is supposed to be the nutty one, but it was me who cracked up after we were married. That awful man trying to kill me didn't help and the Gillett story dragged me down a lot. But I learned from that. I had been naïve. In future, if I had to deliver a message or gift or papers to anyone for Ron and Reg, I'd always take someone with me so no other bastard could make up stories about me.

The morning after the wedding I put on my new brown suede trouser suit and went up to visit Ron. Relationship to patient? it said in the book. 'Wife,' I wrote. I liked that!

Ron was looking good. 'Got any news?' he said. Typical!

It had been a great day for both of us. But what stuck in Ron's mind most of all was walking back to his ward after we'd left for the other reception.

'Kate,' he said, 'me and Charlie had to walk back across the courtyard and it was dark by then. It was brilliant to look up at the stars. It's the first time I've looked up at the stars for more than twenty years. And I'd seen friends and we'd had a few drinks and I was looking at the stars. It was almost like being out again. It was brilliant.'

That put all my own problems into perspective. Things like that remind me of just what Ron's life is like. There are so many things we take for granted – like looking up at a night-time sky.

The memory that is most vivid in my mind is all those photographers, hundreds of them, coming at me, jumping at the bonnet of the Rolls and most of them shouting: 'Why? Why are you marrying him?'

It was weird. I liked it in a way. I think I'd like to be famous – but famous for *me*. That wasn't fame for me. I could have been any old bird. Ron's the one who's famous, not me.

After the visit I went back to Harry's cottage. He was out and I drew the curtains and put the racing on the telly – I love the gee-gees – and I just sat there. I was still in a kind of trance. I couldn't believe I'd done it. I couldn't believe I was Mrs Kray.

Four years on, I wouldn't turn the clock back. I did the right thing, marrying Ron – I know he feels the same. No, we don't sit there in the hall at Broadmoor staring deep into each other's eyes and muttering words of everlasting love. Give me a break! Ron doesn't go in for all that old cobblers. But we look at each other sometimes and we know. We don't have to say anything. People can think what they damn well like. In our own way we love each other and to hell with what people think!

They say the first year of marriage is the worst and that's probably true – even if your husband is miles away banged up in a prison. Or, maybe, especially if your husband is miles away banged up in a prison.

To be fair to Ron, I don't think he realized what I was trying to cope with. Suddenly, wherever I went, out to the pub, to a party, even down to the shops, there would be people going: 'Whisper, whisper. She's married to Ronnie Kray... that's her over there, she's married to Ronnie Kray...'

After a few weeks I began to get really paranoid about it.

I went home to Harry's cottage one day after visiting Ron and as I got out of the car I saw a couple looking through the sitting-room windows. It didn't even occur to me that they might be burglars – they looked more like sightseers.

So I said: 'Can I help you?'

'We're looking for the house where Ronnie Kray's wife lives. It's around here, ain't it?'

'Yes, this is it, I'm her and I suppose you'd better come in and have a cup of tea.'

They turned out to be fans, fans of the Krays, and they'd travelled all the way from Blackpool just to see where I lived! I gave them a cup of tea and a piece of cake and they went away again.

My life changed in ways I could never have imagined. I was looking around for a flat of my own to buy, but suddenly I found it difficult to get a mortgage and the bank treated Kate Kray in a very different way to how they had treated Kate Howard. Suddenly they didn't want to know.

Kate Howard was all right but Kate Kray wasn't a good bet! Of course, as a married woman you always have to put the name of your husband on these forms. And what does he do? they ask you . . . Um!!!

There were little things like trying to claim for any kind of insurance. I used to collect antique china figures of the children of the world. They were Worcester and quite beautiful and often Harry would give me one for my birthday or Christmas.

I kept them on the windowledge at Harry's and one day when I had the window open and it blew shut, one of them fell on to the floor, breaking off its head. They weren't worth much – just a couple of hundred each – but when I rang the insurance company you would have thought I was claiming for the crown jewels! They weren't prepared simply to send me a form – they had to send a man around to the house.

And when I wanted to insure the beautiful wedding ring Ron had given me the insurance premium turned out to be astronomical – just because I was Ron's wife. I couldn't possibly afford it.

On the plus side, becoming a Kray did have a few advantages. Once I was driving along when the police pulled me in for a routine traffic check. The officer looked at my driving licence. Kray.

'No relation to Reg or Ron?' he laughed.

'Yeah, I'm Ron's wife...'

He was fascinated and out came the usual barrage of questions. He quickly forgot why he'd stopped me – a right result, as I had four bald tyres and no tax or insurance at the time!

Of course suddenly some people wanted to know me. And I was photographed by lots of famous photographers, including Lord Lichfield, who took some lovely pictures of me. They're Ron's favourites and he keeps one of them in his room. Before he took the photos he asked me to meet him at his studio in London.

After he had looked at me with a critical but professional eye he said: 'OK, I'll shoot you on Monday.'

'Er, perhaps you'd better rephrase that,' I said. 'Your idea of "shoot" is a bit different to mine.'

He roared with laughter – and so did Ron when I told him.

I was still running the kissagram business – although after being set up I never did a party myself – and the chaffeur business, although I soon gave that up. Ron wasn't keen on the idea of me driving other people around.

On top of that I was also busy looking for a flat – and a building society or bank who would give a Kray a mortgage. Money was becoming a problem. I thought of becoming a croupier. No chance. As soon as they discovered who I was, no one would train me, let alone hire me.

But most of my time was taken up running around for Ron. I was looking after Ron's money for him and, believe me, that's a job in itself. He's the most generous man in the world and as soon as any money comes in it goes straight out again.

Over the years Ron has given away thousands. If a friend is in trouble and writes to Ron he'd never refuse them. And there are all the ordinary people who write to him and tell him how they've fallen on hard times.

'Send him a hundred,' he'd say to me. 'Send her fifty pounds...'

The twins have given thousands to charities over the years, too, and I know he paid for one friend's little girl to have a operation to correct her harelip.

And then there are the gifts...

He'd say: 'Can you go and buy so and so a t-shirt and send it to him... Can you get so and so that CD and post it to him...' Maybe they were gifts for cons in other prisons or maybe friends on the outside. But I'd have to find the t-shirt and the CD and get the wrapping paper and go to the Post Office and express them. There were dozens of jobs like that – at one stage I reckoned we were keeping the Post Office in business! – and of course it all took time and money.

Someone summed it up to me shortly after we got married when they said that before you marry a man he will ask you to do something – after you're married he *tells* you! And I make that right!

I was doing the long drive up to Broadmoor every other day and Ron would say do this and do that and ring him and ring her and tell him this and that.

And life wasn't helped by the silly bastard who boasted on the 'Derek Jameson Show' that he could ring Reggie in prison whenever he liked. 'Well go on,' said Derek, not unreasonably. 'Ring him now.' Naturally he couldn't get through to Reg and it made him look a right idiot.

But after they heard that story at Broadmoor the authorities wouldn't let anyone ring Ron either. So everything had to go through me. I was fixing all his visits and the phone never stopped ringing.

It made me feel so guilty because these lovely friends would ring and say, 'Could you tell the Colonel...' or 'Can I go and visit Ron on Tuesday?' and then they'd launch into long stories about the old days and how it was wicked that the twins were still locked up after all this time and I'd think: 'I'm in the middle of my dinner, I just want my dinner, go away and leave me alone...' which wasn't fair because they were lovely people and good friends of Ron's. But I was getting to the end of my tether.

It got worse and worse. I'd see Ron and he'd say: 'Go and do this and that' . . . and 'Have you done this or that?' And if I hadn't he'd say: 'Well, why haven't you done it?' not realizing I hadn't had the time.

Then I'd go home and I'd hardly walked in the door when Reg would ring and say: 'Could you do this and that and why haven't you done this or that?' And Ron would say: 'I told you to send fifty quid to my friend and I've just heard from him that he still hasn't got it. Why not?'

There were many, many times I remember just sitting down on the floor at home and crying and thinking: 'I've got all these messages and I haven't done them...' and I'd get all muddled up. 'There's just too many... I don't know how I'm going to do them all...' And then I'd worry about money and finding a flat and running the businesses and fixing Ron's visits and if I didn't do it in time Ron wouldn't get a visit.

I couldn't balance it all up. I had lists everywhere and I bought a little book in which I wrote the phone numbers and addresses of all the people, but however hard I tried I was always behind.

It wasn't Ron's fault, it wasn't anyone's fault, it was just me getting into a tizzy. I was trying to do it all and I couldn't. Ron's a real sweetie but he was wearing me out.

I felt as if my life was being taken over. I wasn't me any more. I didn't even look like me any more. One day I looked in the mirror and I hated what I saw. My hair was blonde and long but I hated that too. So, on the spur of the moment, I went to the hairdresser's and told him to cut it all off. He cut it to about a quarter of an inch and I hated it.

So I told him to dye it red. I hated that, too, and so did Ron. When I went to visit him he didn't even recognize me – he walked straight past me.

'My God,' he said, 'what have you done? Get it back to the way it was.'

I went back to the hairdresser's and had it bleached white. But to do that, the hairdresser had to cut it even shorter. I looked a right state. I was obviously not well and, looking back, I didn't like myself or what was happening to me, so I tried to change that by taking it out on my hair of all things.

Then I decided I wanted a tattoo. Don't ask me why. I was just nutty. I told Ron and he joked I should have 'Property of Ronnie Kray' and underneath, 'The Colonel'. I don't think he realized I was seriously going to get one.

No, I knew what I wanted: a hummingbird. I'd seen a tattoo of a hummingbird on a man I'd been 'whipping' during one of my kissagrams and I'd liked it.

Harry reluctantly took me to the tattooist. I was taken into a little room and told to sit in something like a dentist's chair while the man set to work tattooing a hummingbird on my left shoulder. He wouldn't allow Harry in, so he watched what was going on through a window into the room.

'So,' said the tattooist, looking at Harry, 'your husband doesn't mind you having this done?' And he carried on drilling.

'He's not my husband.'

'But I see you're wearing a wedding ring. I can see you're married. Won't your husband mind?'

'He won't know,' I said.

'Where is he?'

'He's in prison.'

'Doing long?'

'Thirty years.'

'Who is he?' he laughed. 'Ronnie or Reggie Kray?!'

'Ronnie, actually.'

The drill stopped. The man's face changed. 'He really

doesn't know that I'm doing this?!'

He looked at me anxiously. I looked at Harry through the window. He was roaring with laughter.

'Carry on,' I said. And he did – bombarding me with questions as everyone does.

All my friends said I'd regret having the tattoo done and admittedly I probably wouldn't have had it done if I hadn't been feeling so weird at the time. But, even now, I don't regret it. I like my hummingbird.

There was something else my friends said. They said I'd changed. I was too busy for them and it seemed as if I didn't care about them any more – that wasn't true, but everything was getting too much for me.

When I went out I always felt people were pointing at me and I was never introduced as Kate any more. It was always: 'This is Ronnie Kray's wife.' And I'd say, 'I'm Kate, I'm me.'

I've quite a strong personality, but I felt as if I was losing my identity. Kate was disappearing and someone else had taken her place, someone I didn't even recognize.

Ron knew I wasn't right. I wasn't my usual self, laughing and joking with him, and I'd lost a lot of weight. I was argumentative and awkward. Sometimes I was quite bitchy to him.

'You need to go and see someone, a doctor,' he said. I didn't take any notice.

Then one day I went to visit him and I was feeling awful. I'd really reached rock-bottom, thanks to a bloody awful story about me that had appeared in a Sunday magazine. It was all so stupid and my own fault, too, which I suppose made it even worse.

I'll explain. Paul Lake, the artist who came to our wedding, had finished his painting of the twins – the horrible one with Ron looking like he'd bitten someone's head off. We'd had 200 prints of the painting done, Ron and Reg had signed them and we planned to sell them off at £200 a time. I agreed to talk to the people at a Sunday magazine so they could do a story about the prints. I didn't want any money: for the interview I just wanted a bit of publicity for the prints so we could sell them and make some cash. 'Sweet,' said Ron. And it was – in theory.

The man from the magazine came down to my house and he turned out to be really nice. Great fun. He was there for five and a half hours and we had a right laugh. He took loads of pictures and we spent hours larking about.

'Have you got any memorabilia from the 1960s?' he said.

'Well,' I said, 'I've got Jack the Hat's hat upstairs with a bullet hole in it!'

His mouth fell open. 'Go and get it!'

'I'm only winding you up!' I said. Jack, of course, wasn't even shot; he was stabbed.

Then we were chatting away and he asked me about Ron's sexuality. Ron's never made any secret of the fact that he's bisexual and has had gay relationships.

'But there's nothing wrong with people being gay,' I said. 'Lots of people are bisexual. In fact, I think most of us are probably bisexual to a certain extent.'

It was a flippant remark. I said it without thinking.

'Are you bisexual?' he asked.

'I suppose so. I mean if it's true that all of us are a bit bisexual I must be, mustn't I?'

They took some smashing pictures to go with the story and I was looking forward to seeing it come out on the Sunday. I was also looking forward to getting a plug for the twins' prints and I had visions of selling the lot in double-quick time and making bundles. That would have cheered Ron up no end.

The Sunday the story came out I was standing in the kitchen and I grabbed the paper as soon as it arrived... And there was the headline screaming at me from the page: 'I'M A GAY KRAY TOO!' I almost fainted. I couldn't believe it. I ripped it up and threw it in the bin. Harry came in to see what was going on.

'You don't want to read it, Harry,' I cried. 'It's horrible!'

I went up to see Ron. He had already read it. I put my hands up. I'd fallen on my arse and that's what I said to him.

'You say all these flippant things and you don't think first. You've *got* to think first, Kate.'

Then he started asking me if I'd done everything he'd asked me to. I told him I'd been trying to do everything but I just couldn't.

'Did you ring the man I asked you to?'

'No.'

'I don't ask you to do much, you could at least do that for me.'

Something in me snapped. I burst into tears. Ron was surprised. He'd rarely seen me in tears before and he's very much a man's man. He hates to see women crying. Like a lot of men, he doesn't know how to cope with it.

'Oh, don't cry,' he said and reached over to wipe my

eyes. That made it worse. He rubbed mascara all down my face.

I ran off to tidy myself up in the ladies'. When I came back things still weren't any better. I tried to explain that it was all getting on top of me, but he didn't listen. We started arguing. It was our first proper row. I got up and left.

I was terribly upset and the screws had never seen me upset before. They were really concerned. 'What's the matter, Kate?' But I couldn't talk. I was in floods of tears. I got in the car and drove off and all the way down the motorway I was crying and crying and my eyes were kind of flickering. I couldn't see properly.

I walked into Harry's and he was worried. 'What on earth's the matter with you?'

But I couldn't talk, all I could do was cry. It got worse. It was as if I was paralysed. I couldn't eat, I kept being sick and I had terrible stomach upsets. And that's how I was for days. It was everything, everything was wrong and it was all too much. The world was closing in on me. I felt trapped and, in a strange way, disorientated.

Harry rang the doctor who came to see me straight away.

'She's having a nervous breakdown,' she said and they wanted to put me into a nursing home in Maidstone. But Harry wouldn't have any of that. He said: 'She's not going there; I'll look after her.' And he did.

It can't have been easy. I was frozen in this terrible state. I couldn't do anything except cry. Harry sent a message to Ron that I wasn't well and he sent me a beautiful bouquet of flowers and the next day one arrived from Reg.

I didn't see Ron for a week, then Harry drove me up. I walked in with no make-up – that must have been a bit of shock for him! – and I looked deadly pale. Ron was sweet. He could see I wasn't well.

'Are you all right? Pull yourself together.' Then: 'Got any news?'

It took me a long while to get better, really better. The doctor wanted me to take tranquillizers, but I wouldn't. I don't even like taking an aspirin. For weeks I didn't answer the phone, I didn't work, Harry took all the messages for me. At one point I couldn't even cope with walking out of the front door. I just hid at home, but slowly I got back to being my old self.

It was a great relief to Ron. He never said much, but he was always telling me to look after myself. He can be a real sweetie when he wants to be. Of course sometimes he can be a right git, but deep down he's a very kind man.

I told him I didn't want to do his money for him any more – I couldn't cope with it. And I told him I couldn't do all Reggie's business as well as his, but Reggie had just got himself a new girlfriend and she was doing most of that, so that was OK.

Gradually life started getting back to normal and, gradually, I managed to get things back into perspective. I vowed to myself that in the future I wasn't going to take it all so seriously. I'd do my best, but I couldn't do more than that. I had been very ill but I'd come out the other side. I think the experience changed me. Some people said it made me harder. I'm not sure. I know that afterwards I felt better in my head and my heart, more in control.

But physically I didn't feel right. One morning I was staying at Harry's and I got out of bed and just collapsed on the floor. I was in agony. Harry got an ambulance and they rushed me into Maidstone hospital.

The doctors found a tumour the size of a baby's head on my womb. It wasn't cancerous, thank God, but it had burst and poisoned my system. I was very poorly so they asked for my next of kin. That, of course, is Ron.

Harry got on to Broadmoor and told them what was happening. The hospital realized who I was, so they put me into a private room – I don't think they wanted anyone to find out I was there and have the press traipsing up and down their wards! As it was, one of the lady patients got a bit of a shock one morning.

Usually they let me keep the telephone trolley in my room so Ron could ring me, but one day someone needed it on the ward. The phone rang and the lady patient answered it.

'Hello,' said a voice. 'Reggie Kray here! Can I speak to Kate?'

'I'm sorry,' she said. 'This is Maidstone hospital.'

'Yeah, it's Reg Kray here. That you, Kate? Got any news? How are you?'

When I was feeling a bit better, I met the woman in the corridor. 'We thought you must be here,' she said. 'Because we kept seeing these big men in the corridors. There's never been any gangsters visiting before.'

Gangsters? That was just Harry and my friend, Pa!

At one stage I was so ill they thought I was going to die. Ron was worried and there was talk of him coming to see me, maybe for the last time. But the press knew I was there by this time and it would have been mayhem. It wasn't worth him coming. The last time the public knew he was out was at Violet's funeral in 1982, and I didn't want to put him through all that again. It was a circus.

So we spoke as often as we could on the phone. I was feeling very weak, but Ron still managed to make me smile.

'Got any news? Now, I know you're not feeling very well but can you phone so and so . . .'

And there was I, lying flat on my back with all these drips in my arms and wired up to all these monitors!

But he sent me some lovely flowers and letters, not saying much, just: 'My dear Kate, I'm glad you're feeling better. I'm looking forward to seeing you soon. Keep your chin up, God bless, Love from Ron xxxxx. Don't worry, we'll soon have bundles of money! Ha, ha!'

At the back of my mind, even after breaking up with Harry and marrying Ron, I think there was always this little tiny spark of hope that maybe, just maybe, I might one day have a baby of my own. My head knew that was daft. My head knew I'd never have a baby of my own, but it's funny, isn't it? Even when you know there's no hope, you go on secretly hoping.

I had talked to Ron about having children. At one point I even considered adopting a baby, but it didn't work out. He's never been keen to have children. He says that when he gets out he has a lot of catching up to do and he won't have time for all that.

But he likes kids. He's godfather to Alex, Wilf Pine's little boy, who's about eight now. He was christened in

Broadmoor and I know that Ron was really pleased to be godfather. He sends Alex birthday cards and a bit of money at birthdays and Christmas, all the usual things, but he's not soppy about children.

He's not the sort of man who'd go gooey over babies and pick them up and let them puke all over his suit or have a little kiddie come up and sit on his lap. He's more the type to pat him on the head and say: 'Good kid, have a lolly' and then turn to the grown-ups: 'Got any news?'

But with me it was different. When I was a little stronger, and fit to be operated on, my lovely doctor, Dr Kefford, came to see me. Funnily enough even he had a story about the twins – he said he'd met them in a club in the 1960s.

I knew what he was going to say and he knew that I knew. He was going to tell me that I'd never have kids.

I think he understood – as much as any man can understand – how bad I felt, but it's funny how you react in circumstances like that. He was trying to explain to me about the state of my insides.

'Your ovaries have become like my testicles,' he said.

'What, all hairy?' I said.

'No,' he laughed. 'I mean enlarged.'

But it was no joke, really, and we both knew it. A couple of days later he performed the hysterectomy and my dream of having kids was over once and for all.

Physically I feel brilliant now as long as I remember to take my Hormone Replacement Therapy. But the emptiness is still there. You just get used to living with it.

After about three weeks in hospital, I began to feel better. All I wanted to do was get out. I went back to

Harry's to recuperate, then Harry told me about a flat he'd seen. It was really lovely, in a quiet road near the centre of town, but there were fields all around and a river at the end of the garden so you felt you were really in the depths of the country.

I fell in love with it straight away. It was going to be my own place. Somewhere I could just be me, a place no one could find me unless I wanted them to. Sod it, I thought, I'll buy it. And I did.

Ron was pleased. The papers knew Harry's address and phone number but only Ron and really close friends and family know about the flat. It's mine. Ron knows I have to have somewhere to get away from it all.

So I moved in, and life fell into a kind of routine. I wasn't visiting Ron every other day any more. He understood. It was just too much. But I'd go up two or three times a week and we were getting on better than ever. We feel easy with each other and we make each other laugh. Sometimes he can be so comical.

'I'm going to become a vegetarian,' he said to me during that scare about mad-cow disease.

'What on earth for?'

'If you eat beef you can go mad.'

'Well, you're bloody mad already, otherwise you wouldn't be here, would you, so what are you worried about?'

Ron roared with laughter. 'Yeah, I hadn't looked at it like that. But don't you eat beef, Kate...'

Sometimes we laugh so much we cry with laughter. And of course we have our rows like any other couple.

'I'm bloody leaving!!!' I've said to him during some ruck or other.

'I'm bloody well staying here!' he's said back.

'Well, you don't have much bloody choice, do you!!!'

We usually end up smiling. It's a funny relationship, but it's good.

Even so, I'd still sit at home and there was something missing. What was it?... I knew, of course. A man. Ron is affectionate and we have a little kiss and a cuddle but... I hadn't been to bed with a man for over two years. Two years! I don't think celibacy is good for people. And now I was feeling better...

## CHAPTER SIX

# *Sex and All That . . .*

I lost my virginity on the green baize of a pool table at the local youth club when I was thirteen. The pool tables were downstairs and there was a room upstairs where they used to hold dances. A really good club it was – I was a skinhead at the time.

Andy and I had been dancing away at the club and then he persuaded me to go downstairs with him. One thing led to another and while we did it on the table I could hear Bob Marley singing 'No Woman No Cry' upstairs. Or was it Smokey Robinson and 'Wherever I Hang My Hat'?

Maybe because of the music I wasn't giving Andy my full attention, or maybe he simply wasn't very good at it – after all, he was only fourteen! But afterwards I remember thinking: 'Well, is that *it*?' I was not impressed. 'A lot of fuss about nothing,' I thought.

But I was very young, too; and like most of us, as I got older sex grew on me!

I've never been promiscuous and I've never gone in for one-night stands. I've always been at least a little in love. First, there was Andy. He never believed he was the first, but he was. For years there was Andy, then there were others, I admit – but always I was a little in love. Then for thirteen years there was Harry.

I've never had any hang-ups about sex. Sex is OK.

Sex is good for you. A happy sex life makes life much brighter. And, after being married for a year and a half and going without for two and a half, I have to admit I missed it.

What people don't understand is that Ron understands. When people meet me and hear that I'm married to Ron the first thing that goes through their mind is: How you can have a proper marriage with no sex?

But marriage is about more than sex – it's about love and friendship as much as it's about sex – ask anyone who's been happily married for years. A good sex life is just the icing on the cake.

I'm not saying that Ron and I are just good friends – we're not. It's much more than that. But why do people assume that if you don't have sex you can't have a good relationship and love each other?

There are all kinds of love. There's the love between a mum and her kids, there's the love between sisters and brothers – Ronnie and Reggie love each other – there's the love between friends. All relationships are different and unique and what right does anyone have to say that a relationship isn't special because it doesn't fit in with their own conventional rules?

Just as people are confused about my marriage to Ron, they're almost as baffled by the relationship Harry and I have now.

'*KRAY BRIDE'S LIVE-IN PACT WITH HER EX*' went the headline.

And the story: 'Gangland killer Ronnie Kray's new wife is at the centre of a bizarre marriage triangle. Former strip-o-gram girl Kate Kray wed Ronnie just five months ago – but while he stays locked up in Broadmoor she shares a tiny country cottage with her ex-husband.'

Harry told them: 'We have been friends for a long time and we always will be. Ronnie knows that.'

Bizarre marriage triangle? What rubbish! Apart from Ron, Harry's my best friend. I love him but I'm not in love with him and he feels the same way about me. Sometimes I stay at his cottage but that doesn't mean we sleep together. Harry has his own girlfriends and I always make sure I make myself scarce when they come to stay.

And I was ever so upset by that story that I was a lesbian. I'm not. I've never slept with a woman in my life, or fancied a woman for that matter. 'Kate recently admitted to a string of lesbian affairs...' they wrote. Not true, I did no such thing.

But I still stick by what I said about gays. What's wrong with being gay? If people aren't hurting anyone else, then what's wrong with it? And I think there is a bit of the bisexual in all of us – you can have affection for someone of the same sex even if you don't sleep with them. I'm sure that many of the men who speak out the loudest against homosexuality are the ones who are most afraid of their own sexual feelings.

Ron isn't gay – he's bisexual, and he's never made any secret of it. And if you're bisexual, you can't change that, just as you can't change the colour of your eyes. He told me he lost his virginity when he was sixteen to a girl in the East End but, he says, he doesn't remember much about it!

Then he had girlfriends. There was one lovely girl called Monica he was seeing before he was sent away. She later married and took her new husband to see Ron in prison. There were girlfriends and, yes, there were boyfriends. Everyone knows that Ron likes young men. So what? That's his business and no one else's.

Sexual relationships aren't allowed in prison and anyone caught having a sexual relationship in Broadmoor would find themselves in trouble. All kinds of privileges are taken away from you. There was a ludicrous story that rent boys had visited Ron in Broadmoor to have sex with him. Some people have a vivid imagination. He's always watched by at least six 'nurses' during visits and the idea that he could take these boys off for hours on end to have sex with them is ridiculous. Anyway, Ron has far too much self-respect to carry on like that.

Ron doesn't have sexual relationships with any of the men and women he lives with in Broadmoor, but over the years he has made several good friends. A good thing, too. Everyone needs friendship and affection. Everybody needs somebody.

All his adult life, both men and women have been attracted to Ron. He is very charming and he has a wicked smile. And there's an aura about him, an aura of danger. Over the years he's been visited by some young men – and young women. They write to him and he invites them up to see him. He enjoys their company – and he enjoys a little flirt. Who doesn't? He also enjoys teasing me about them. 'You old git,' I say, and he roars with laughter.

But usually these friendships don't last very long – a few weeks, a month or two.

Ron jokes about these passing friendships.

'You know I enjoy my little "flings"', he says. 'But you know you're my number one, Kate.'

Of course some inmates do have sex with each other in prison. Many men who were totally heterosexual on the outside end up having a homosexual love affair inside. But if a man with a normal healthy sex drive is banged up with a load of men and no women for years and years on end, what do you expect? They're looking for some love and affection, to feel close to someone. In some states of America they have recognized the problem and long-term prisoners are allowed special days with their wives to sustain their relationships.

Before Ron and I got married we talked about his first marriage to Elaine Mildener. It didn't last very long – I don't know if Elaine could cope. You have to be strong to be married to Ron. She didn't have much money and she also had two kids to look after.

Before our wedding, through a good friend of ours, Gel Charles, I arranged to visit Elaine. Ron wasn't keen on the idea. Like most men, he prefers to keep his women separate! But I was curious. A second wife is always curious about the first. It's natural.

We had tea and I liked her, although she was very different to me.

'What did you think of her?' Ron asked.

'She's nice.'

'Yeah, she is,' he said. End of conversation.

Before we married we also talked about sex, of course we did. We still do, for that matter.

One day on a visit he surprised me by telling me he'd had an AIDs test.

'Why?' I said.

'Just to put your mind at rest,' he said.

'You didn't have to do that.'

'I know,' he said. 'But I thought you might have wondered – and I knew you wouldn't ask me.'

Ron can be very considerate sometimes. Mind you, at the same time he also suggested I sign a marriage contract saying I wouldn't take half of everything he had if we got divorced! Cheek! 'Half of what?' I said. 'I've got as much as you!' He laughed and the contract was forgotten.

We talked about me and other men. Ron's not daft. And he's not a selfish man. He knows I'm young, I'm healthy, I'm normal. We don't know when he's going to come out and there's no way he'd expect me to give up boyfriends while he's inside.

But of course there are ground rules. At least, he has only one and that's: Don't take liberties! That's fair enough and Ron knows I never would anyway. I have too much respect for him.

Everything Ron said to me before our marriage I agreed with wholeheartedly. If I was going to have an affair he didn't want me to have a boyfriend who thought that, by being with me, he was somehow getting one over on Ron. In fact, Ron was far more worried about someone taking advantage of me because I was Mrs Kray than anything else. Because no one takes a liberty with Ron – not ever.

Ron didn't want some bloke making passes at me just because I was married to him and me getting hurt in the process. If I went out with anyone he said he didn't want me to take him to the clubs and pubs in London that his friends use. 'If you do have a relationship with someone – don't flaunt it.'

And he didn't want me going out, on dates or in a romantic way, with his friends. Fair enough. He wasn't worried about himself. He was worried about me and he was worried that some of his friends might not understand that Ron thought it was OK for me to have men friends. *They* might think the man was taking a liberty and, without asking Ron, do something naughty.

Above all, Ron wanted me to be happy. But it was all very well that Ron and I had agreed everything and all very well that Ron had given me permission to have men friends – I had to find one first!

Once I felt better after my illnesses I used to moan to Ron that I didn't have anyone to take me out. Harry's brilliant, but he's not a boyfriend and, anyway, he has his own girlfriends and his own life to lead.

And being Mrs Kray has definite disadvantages if you're looking for a boyfriend – not that I ever went out of my way to search for one.

I soon found out that being married to Ronnie Kray had a strange effect on men! If one of Ron's acquaintances fancied me he wouldn't do anything, or take it any further and ask me out, out of respect for Ron. And the ones who didn't know Ron wouldn't take it any further, or ask me out, out of fear of Ron. So, either way, I'd had it – or rather I hadn't!

Most of the time after we married the only parties I went to were get-togethers for Ron's friends. I'm naturally chatty and like having fun, and I'd be at a party having a good laugh with someone when suddenly a friend would whisper in his ear: 'That's Ronnie's wife' and abracadabra! They'd disappear in a cloud of smoke!

I remember being at one party and no one would even ask me and the girl I was with to dance. I told Ron. He roared with laughter. 'That's because you two were the ugliest girls there!' he said.

Then one day I went to another do and I was standing at the bar having an orange juice and talking to some friends and suddenly in walked this gorgeous man. Cor! I thought. Now, he *is* handsome...

Our eyes met across the room and I tried to act cool. But I knew, just as you always do, that he'd come over and ask to buy me a drink. So I stood there trying not to look at him and he was over the other side of the room trying not to look at me and finally he came over.

'Can I buy you a drink?'

My brother-in-law Charlie came bouncing over, bless him, and said, 'Have you met our Ron's wife?' The man took hold of my hand and held it hard. We looked at each other.

'Hello,' he said. And then, quietly, 'Sorry.'

He turned out to be the son of one of Ron's oldest business acquaintances.

Of course I told Ron all about it – I tell him everything – and as we walked out of the hall he was laughing. 'You've got good taste, Kate,' he said. 'I liked him myself once!'

It became a standing joke. I'd be out with Harry and his girlfriend, feeling a bit of a gooseberry, and some nice bloke would get chatting to me and then I'd pop to the

Ladies' and I'd say, 'I bet you a tenner that when I come back, you'll have gone.'

'No way,' he'd say.

But while I was out of sight someone would say, 'That's Ronnie Kray's wife.' And the bloke would be off like a shot.

But with Pa it was different. Sometimes in life I'm sure you're fated to be with someone and that's how it was with me and Pa. I always called him Pa, short for Grandpa, because he was always moaning. He was a friend of Harry's, and I first met him when Harry and I were still married way back in 1981. I take marriage seriously and I was never unfaithful to Harry and I always told him everything, still do.

Pa was a car dealer and I first clapped eyes on him when I was delivering some parts to his garage. Six foot something, half Spanish, jet-black hair swept back and soft, soft eyes. The first thing I thought was: 'God, he's so handsome!'

He looked at me and he was looking at me the way I was looking at him. 'What time do you finish work?' he said. 'Can I take you out to tea?'

He picked me up in this huge American car and we went out to tea. We never touched each other, we never slept with each other, but after that he was always phoning me up and asking me out. He chased me all over Dartford! He didn't leave me alone. It was flattering. And I was tempted. But there was Harry. I loved Harry. I'd never be unfaithful to Harry.

I didn't know what to do. So I did what I always do – I asked Harry. He was sitting in the bath when I got home and I sat on the edge while I told him about my feelings for Pa.

Harry, as usual, was straight and sensible.

'I'm not in love with him. But I fancy him...'

'Well,' said Harry. 'It's your life and your decision. I want you to stay with me but if you want this man you have to leave me. You can't have both of us.'

Harry or Pa? I stayed with Harry, so that was that and Harry and I soon moved down to Maidstone. Pa and I saw each other only once in the next ten years. Harry was selling Pa a car.

'Let me come, let me come...' So I went along too and there he was with his wife and a baby and he looked at me and I looked at him and we didn't say a word. We didn't have to.

Then two years ago I was at Harry's cottage. Married to Ron now, better, bored, thinking... It was February and it was a Tuesday.

Harry knew what I was thinking. 'Go on,' he said, 'ring him.' And he gave me Pa's number.

'I can't, I can't...'

'Go on.'

'I can't... Can I?'

And what could I say to a man I hadn't really seen for ten years? Well, he was in the car business... I *could* say I was looking for a car to buy... I took a deep breath and rang.

He picked up the phone almost on the first ring, so I had no chance of chickening out.

'Hello.'

'Is that Pa?' I said, feeling nervous. 'It's Kate.

I'm looking for a Jaguar, a blue XJS.' I knew he dealt in high-performance cars and it was the first thing that entered my mind.

So we started chatting about cars, but he sounded awkward so I said: 'Can't you talk?'

'Not really.'

He took my number and said he'd ring me the following morning, which he did from a call box.

'Sorry I couldn't talk last night,' he said. 'I'm still in shock that you rang.'

I carried on the pretence about the car and he said he'd visit a garage he knew where he thought he might be able to get hold of one for me at a good price. I couldn't believe I was really doing this. I never chase after men, never! Besides, I knew he was married. But I didn't care.

We arranged to meet the following evening at the station car park and then he'd take me to see an XJS. I was early and waited in my car for him. Then I saw this big Yankee car pull in and I knew it was him. He always did drive flash cars.

I wasn't looking my best. My hair had grown a bit after the time I had it all cut off, and it was no longer dyed red, I was back to my normal blonde. Even so, I probably looked odd.

But Pa didn't seem to notice. I got into his car and we just sat there smiling at each other. Then we started talking about cars until I saw he was wearing this big heavy bracelet just like Jimmy Savile's. I started to laugh and he pushed it up his sleeve.

I said: 'Do you want to go for a drink?'

He said: 'Do you want to see the car?'

I said: 'Car? What car? Let's go for a drink.'

We drove to a really quiet country pub where we wouldn't meet anyone either of us knew and then we sat and talked and it was as if the last ten years had never happened. The spark was still there. And I kept looking at him and thinking: 'You've got nice eyes!'

And he still felt the same about me. I knew he'd always had this thing for me. Unfortunately, his wife knew it too. He told me that when I married Ron he went home that evening and his wife threw the paper at him and said: 'See who your girlfriend's married now!'

He was shocked, he said. He couldn't believe that I'd divorced Harry and married Ron.

So we talked and talked and suddenly I blurted out: 'Do you want to be my boyfriend?' And then I thought: 'Did I really say that?' But I had to be straight with him. There was no point in beating around the bush. I wanted him. I wanted him very much but I had to think of Ron. Pa was someone I knew I could trust totally. He wouldn't be with me just because I was Mrs Kray and he wouldn't be with me and then run to the papers.

Pa was a bit taken aback. 'But what about Ron?' he said. 'Wouldn't he mind?'

'I'd have to tell Ron,' I said. 'I'd never do anything to mug him off or embarrass him.'

Pa just looked at me. 'I couldn't believe it when you rang. I put the phone down and thought, "Nah, it wasn't her. I'm dreaming."' Then he leaned across the little wooden table in the pub and kissed me.

Oh yes, I thought, oh yes. We looked at each other.

'Gimme another kiss,' I said, laughing.

'Let's have another drink!' he said.

We left the pub and he put his arms around me. It was like I was alive again. He drove me back to my car and I drove home to Harry's feeling *great*! Harry was pleased for me. 'But what about his wife?' he said, and: 'You've got to tell Ron.'

Of course. In fact I couldn't wait to tell Ron. He's my best friend, apart from anything else, and I knew he'd be happy for me. I knew we could both trust Pa.

Pa rang the next morning. 'Am I dreaming?' he said. 'Are you having me on?'

'No, honest.'

'Can I see you tonight?'

I was excited, but I was wary too. We couldn't go anywhere I might be recognized in case someone tipped off the papers. I couldn't do that to Ron. I'd die rather than do that to Ron. I had to be very, very careful. No one must know.

I agreed to see Pa but I also decided that I wouldn't sleep with him for a while. I wanted to talk to Ron first. Besides, I didn't want Pa to think I'd just picked him up to have sex with him. I've never been like that. Harry says I'm a prude – I'm not, but I'm not a slag either!

Pa took me out for a meal to a quiet country restaurant. He put a tape on in his car – it was the Commodores, 'Three Times a Lady'. It was lovely. Pa is very romantic.

Then he pulled a piece of paper out of his pocket. 'Remember this?' he said. It was a telegram I'd sent him way back, telling him I couldn't go out with him. He'd kept it all those years. It was a lovely evening.

The next day I hurried up to Broadmoor to see Ron.

'Got any news?' he said.

Then he grinned. 'You look better!'

I grinned back. Ron knows me well.

'I know,' I said. 'I've got something to tell you.'

'Ah, you've had sex?!'

'No!'

'What then?'

So I told him all about Pa.

'You remember the bloke I told you about from years ago?'

'Vaguely . . .'

'Look, I wouldn't mug you off, you know that . . .'

'It's all right . . . I don't mind. . . .'

Then Ron got serious. 'I don't want him to go to London with you and don't take him where any of my friends go. I don't want it broadcast. And I *don't* want to read about it in the papers.'

'Of course not.' I paused. 'Ron, he's married.'

'I'm not sure you should be involved with a married man. You'll have to be careful, be discreet. Are you sure you know what you're doing? Don't worry about me. You're only young and I'd be a fool to think you weren't going to see anyone else. And I want you to be happy.'

Ron loves me but he loves me in his own way. I agreed we'd be careful and Ron thought I would cope. He knows I can take care of myself. He doesn't like fluffy women around him. All the women in his life have been strong: his mother, his Aunt Rose, the women he's loved. You've got to be strong to be around the twins and Ron, especially, couldn't cope with all that crap of someone playing the silly little woman.

I know it's one of the things he likes about me. Ron could have married a hundred women before I came along – he's always getting women writing to him, buttering him up and even proposing. But he liked me because I'm not like that and I am strong. I'm a grafter, he says.

He likes people who are straightforward and honest. He expects people to go out and live life, earn their own living, do a bit of business... It's always business before anything. Women should always be looked after – but they should be able to look after themselves too. So Ron wasn't worried. He knows I can look after myself and he trusts me.

Even so, he was curious...

'What's he like, then?'

I showed him a photo of Pa.

'He's really young,' I teased him. 'And he's got this lovely skin, a sort of olivey colour, he's really handsome.'

Ron studied the picture. 'Looks like a gypsy boy.' And he's called him that ever since.

Soon Pa and I were seeing each other every Friday. Then it was Fridays and Wednesdays. Then it was Fridays, Wednesdays and Sundays. On Friday nights we'd go to a club and dance all night but we never went to a London club out of respect for Ron. We'd go to Folkestone or somewhere like that. And still I didn't sleep with him. He'd put his arms around me and we'd kiss but I'd always drop him back at his car. Pa likes a drink but he won't drink and drive and I don't drink anyway.

We didn't rush into bed with each other. We wanted it to be special. I didn't have my own place then so I wasn't going to take him back to Harry's – that would have been a liberty. And I wouldn't do that to Harry.

So we waited. Pa said: 'If we're going to do it we're going to do it properly.'

And I agreed.

So he booked a hotel in Brighton and we drove down there one Friday afternoon. Even then we waited. We left our bags in the room and went for a long walk along the seafront and then to the pictures and saw *Terminator 2*.

Then I had a bath and changed and all the time I was walking round the room Pa would look at me and smile or stroke my hair.

But still we didn't pounce on each other. We wanted to save it. We didn't want it all over in a few minutes.

We went to a club and danced the night away and then we came back to the room. I wasn't nervous. I was excited. Everything in me wanted this man. Pa picked me up in his arms and laid me on the bed, just like in the movies. Then, very slowly, he undressed me and we made love all night.

The next morning I felt great! Wicked! I would have been happy to stay there in that bed for a week, but we had to go home. And Pa had to ring his wife.

He came out of the phone box while I waited in the car. 'Seagulls,' he said.

'What?'

'Seagulls. She might have heard the seagulls – and I said I was at my mum's – miles from the sea!'

'You've done this before, haven't you?' I said, but I didn't care.

Harry was pleased to see me. He knew where I'd been

– Harry always knows where I am. He looks after me and he was pleased for me but he warned me to be careful. If the press found out... Or Pa's wife!

I went to see Ron in Broadmoor straight away. He was sitting at his usual table as I walked in. He smiled at me.

'You've got a sparkle in your eye,' he said, and gave me a quizzical look.

I punched the air and laughed. 'Yes!'

He said: 'You didn't!'

I said: 'I did!'

He laughed. He was happy for me. He knew it was a good thing. I wasn't any good for Ron when I was ill and now I was definitely feeeling better.

Ron and I understand each other. I don't know if he told Reggie I'd got a boyfriend. I certainly didn't. Reggie might have thought it was taking a liberty. But Ron didn't think like that. And in a way it made our relationship stronger. He understood that I needed a life outside the Krays, some kind of love and affection. I think he also understood what I went through with the nervous breakdown. After all, Ron has suffered mental illness for much of his life so he could understand how I was feeling in a way that not many other people could. Even when I had all my hair cut off I think he was probably the only person who understood why I did it.

Pa and I saw each other every week and he rang me three times a day. Often we'd go out dancing and then we'd go to a hotel. We'd dance and dance for hours and then we'd drive and find somewhere to stay.

Once we were a bit stoned in the early hours and we were driving along near the seafront at Brighton when we saw this big fat man in a vest putting empty milk bottles out on his doorstep. In our haze we thought it was a hotel and asked him if he had a room for the night.

He said yes and showed us to a room. I thought it was a bit funny because it looked as if there were people's personal belongings there, but the room was clean and the bed freshly made so we fell into bed, made love and went to sleep. The next morning we woke up to realize it wasn't a hotel at all. It was the man's private house! We did laugh.

I saw Ron as usual two or three times a week. He didn't want to know about me and Pa. As long as I was happy he was happy.

It was always: 'Got any news?' as usual. And just occasionally:

'How's the gypsy boy? Are you still seeing him?'

'Yes,' I told him.

We even went to America together. It was very spur-of-the-moment. Pa's sister was going there on holiday. She's always known about Pa's feelings for me and we like each other. She's a right nice girl. Pa and I drove her and her husband to the airport for their flight and suddenly she said: 'Why don't you two come over and join us for a couple of weeks?'

We looked at each other. Why not? So Pa got the tickets and I went off to get myself a passport. The queue at the Petty France passport office was a mile long, then when I finally got to the head of the queue the man looked at my form. He looked at my name. He looked at me.

'Sorry,' he said. 'I can't give you your passport because the photo's got to be signed by a professional person.'

'But I'm meant to be going in two days!'

'Don't worry,' he said, 'come back tomorrow and you won't have to queue – just come straight up to my window and I'll make sure the passport's ready for you. And don't tell your husband – I don't want to upset him!' I just smiled.

So I got our local policeman, Dave, to sign my photo – he knows me quite well, and not just because of who I'm married to. There was also the small matter of when I accidentally crashed my BMW into the village bowls club at two in the morning...!

I collected my passport with no trouble at all and I didn't have to queue up again. We had a wonderful time in California. I loved the place – one day, I've decided, I'm going to live there.

But Pa was beginning to get me down. He was becoming increasingly jealous and possessive. We'd be sitting in a restaurant and I'd be innocently looking around when suddenly Pa would say: 'Why are you looking at that man?'

'What man? I wasn't.'

'You were. What, do you fancy him?'

'No, don't be ridiculous.'

If I was driving the car and I waved someone else on he'd go mad. 'Why are you waving at that man?'

When we came back from America it was worse than ever. He didn't like me wearing trendy clothes which were too revealing, and I couldn't look at another man – which was daft because I wasn't interested in anyone else anyway. He wanted to know where I was every hour of every day.

'He's obssessed,' said Harry.

I talked it over with Ron. He said he thought it was a bloody cheek for Pa to be so possessive and he warned me: 'Jealousy is like an illness, Kate. He won't change. Be careful.'

Pa was jealous of my friends, jealous of Harry, jealous of Ron, jealous of anyone and everyone I knew. If I was going out to lunch with some friends he'd say: 'If there's any men there you're not to kiss them hello.' It was getting ridiculous and it was getting me down. I was fond of him, and most of the time I loved being with him, but I couldn't be having all of this.

Pa's jealous rages were driving me crazy. One day I met him and I was wearing a short black skirt and thick black opaque tights. He went mad, completely mad.

'Don't show yourself off like that! Why are you wearing clothes like that?'

'Because it's the fashion, because I like this skirt, because I WANT to!!!'

A few days later I visited Ron wearing the same outfit. Ron always notices clothes and he likes me to be fashionable.

'You look really nice today,' he said.

'Pa doesn't like me in this.'

'Cheek,' said Ron. He was annoyed.

Now I didn't know what to do, the situation was getting out of control. I finished with Pa. I told him I couldn't take his jealousy any more and that I wouldn't see him again. But soon he'd ring up and apologize and promise never to do it again. I have to admit that I felt a bit lonely at times and I was very fond of him, so I'd agree to see him. Then it would happen all over again.

I knew he didn't really want to be like that, but he couldn't help himself. I wanted to help him. I even took him to Relate, the marriage guidance people. I wasn't sure that Pa would come with me – and I certainly wasn't going to go without him – but he agreed.

He even opened up and talked while we were there. The counsellor who saw us was very good and talked us through Pa's jealousy problem. Apparently he's always been like this with the women in his life: he wants to possess them completely and utterly. But no one person can do that to another.

Relate didn't help much. As Harry said, how could they? We went under different names and we couldn't tell the man the whole truth about the situation, so it was difficult for him to guide us.

'It's an illness,' said Ron. 'At the end of the day if you want to go out with him then it's up to you. But remember you don't have to, Kate, you have the choice.'

Harry had a word with Pa and it was OK for a while. But basically nothing could change him. Then came the final straw.

It was Sunday tea-time when I got the call. Pa had been on the drink all day. He'd been chased by the police, dumped the car and now he was at his sister's house. Would I come and get him?

I had no make-up on, I was tired and I hadn't taken my hormone pill. Ever since my hysterectomy if I don't take my hormone pill every day I feel terrible and I can quite literally go bloody mad.

I got to his sister's and there he was, drunk as ten men,

on the sofa. I'd had enough of this. I managed to get him in the car and then he started. My friend's Rayban sunglasses were in the car.

'Where have you been? Whose are these:'

'Virginia's.'

He snatched them, snapped them in half and threw them out of the window. I was furious.

'How dare you!' I said and braked hard so the car screeched to a halt. 'Get out!'

He wouldn't so I kicked him in the face! Still he wouldn't get out, so I got out of the car and went around and opened his door and kicked him again. This time he got out. He grabbed me and I fell against a van.

By this time the traffic was building up – I'd stopped right in the middle of the road. I had the car keys in my hand so I stabbed him with them, got back in the car and drove off.

But I was mad, really mad, and I kept thinking: 'How dare he!' So I turned the car around. I saw him walking up the hill, I went straight for him and ran him over. I drove back down the hill and looked in my rear-view mirror. Something came over me. No, that wasn't enough. So I turned the car again and went back and ran him over again!

Then I went really mad. I got out of the car and there was a wooden stake lying by the side of the road. I picked it up and began to beat him. I promise you I'm not a violent person. I never have been, but something in me snapped. By now the police had arrived and they pulled me off him. Good job too, I think I could have killed him.

They arrested me and carted me off to the police

station. I gave a false name. I didn't want Ron to hear about this. He would have been livid – both at Pa and at me for making such an exhibition of myself. I was madder than hell and they put me in a cell to calm down. Two hours later I had and they let me go. They asked Pa if he wanted to press charges but, not surprisingly, he said no.

I went and found Harry at the pub and told him what had happened. He was horrified and I was so ashamed. It just wasn't like me, but the situation with Pa had been building up and it was driving me truly crazy. Harry went to have a word with Pa. This was getting out of hand. This had to stop.

'Christ,' said Harry. 'You should have seen the state of him! What on earth did you do to him? His face was black and blue!'

I went to the doctor's and said I needed a higher dose of hormones. 'Have you noticed any mood swings?' she asked me. 'Have you found yourself doing anything out of character?'

Mood swings?! Out of character?! 'Well,' I said, 'I've never run anyone over before!' She put me on the highest dose of hormones that you're allowed.

Things changed for me and Pa after that. I was married. He was married. We wanted more but it was impossible for us both. There are people you love – but you can't have, for all sorts of reasons. And that doesn't stop you loving them – ever.

I can't see me ever leaving Ron.

He loves me in his own way and he likes me. He's loyal to me and I'm loyal to him. I always will be. He's not a soppy man – I tell him he's a ruthless bastard. But he can be very thoughtful.

Once we were rowing about some stupid thing – nothing very important. Probably I'd forgotten to do one of his messages or something and he got annoyed and I was in a bad mood.

'Right! RIGHT!' I said. 'I'm going!'

'You're mad,' he said. 'You've gone mad!' Then I stomped off.

The next day Ron rang me. 'Are you coming up to see me Tuesday?'

'I don't know. You weren't very nice to me.' I was sulking.

'I can't help it,' he says. 'It's the German in me!' And I laughed. How can you be mad at someone when they say something like that.

So of course I went up to see him. I can never sulk for long.

'You old bastard,' I said. And he laughed.

'Oh come on,' he says. 'Sit down or I'll smack your arse. Come on, me old dutch . . .' which is what he always calls me but only ever in a matter-of-fact way, not in a gooey sort of way. And then he gives me that look and smiles and you can't be cross with him, you just can't.

If he wants to get me going he reminds me of all the women who write to him. Ron gets about fifty letters a day and most of those are from women. And some of the letters are a bit saucy!

Some women even send rude pictures of themselves. Ron caught me unawares one day.

'So and so sent me some snaps,' he said with a wicked grin. 'Do you want to see them?'

I thought perhaps the girl had been on holiday and these were her holiday snaps.

'Yeah, OK,' I said, not the slightest bit interested. Holiday snaps? You must be joking! There she was, on a bed somewhere in next to nothing and all I could think of to say was: 'Look, she's wearing Marks and Sparks knickers and she can't even be bothered to tuck the label in...'

There's another woman in particular who is always making out she's a special friend of Ron's. I'd like to bloody strangle her. Every now and then Ron winds me up, telling me she's been to see him. He thinks it's very funny when I get the needle.

But we never fall out for long. Occasionally I play up and get a bit moody with him and tell him: 'You don't care about me, you just don't care!'

Then the next day the florist is on the doorstep with a beautiful bunch of flowers and a card from Ron saying, 'I do care, love Ron.'

We talk about sex sometimes – what married couple doesn't? – and we have a bit of a laugh about our conjugal rights. In fact, there's been talk at Broadmoor that some patients who are preparing to start life again on the outside might be allowed to spend the night with their wives.

There's a little house in the grounds – I think Jimmy Savile used to use it when he visited the patients and stayed overnight. It's empty now and they've been thinking of allowing it to be used by the patients to help them to readjust to normal life.

We'd love that. Yes, of course we'd sleep together. But apart from the inevitable it would just be nice to be on our own for a while. We could talk without all those prying eyes and I could cook him a meal.

Not that I'm a great cook. Some time ago the Governor allowed patients to have food brought in for them occasionally.

Ron loves good, old-fashioned English home cooking.

'You know what I'd like,' he said. 'You know what I'd really love . . . a good-home made beef stew with real dumplings.'

'Right,' I said. 'I'll make you one.'

Well, as I said, cooking isn't exactly one of my greatest accomplishments. I'm not a great cook – but I know a couple who are . . . Marks and Spencer. So I bought two of their beef stews with dumplings, unpacked them into a Tupperware thing and took them up to Ron.

He loved them – and he told people: 'My wife makes a lovely stew!'

What a wicked woman!

So I can just see me, if they allow us to spend a night together in that little house, staggering up the path loaded down with Marks and Sparks food – in Tupperware containers!

But who knows if that will ever happen? I hope so. We might be an odd couple – but we are a couple.

Everyone is always asking me why I married Ron. Why, why, why? It drives me around the bend. But no one's ever asked Ron why he married Kate, have they? Recently one of his little girlfriends who goes up to see him suggested he divorce me and marry her!

Ron, I'm pleased to say, would have none of it.

'Kate's my wife,' he said. 'The number one.'

But then I asked him: 'Why did you marry me?'

'It was good looks to start with,' Ron told me. 'You're pretty and you've got a nice figure and I was attracted by that. And you're always laughing – and *not* a nag! And we seemed to be able to relate to one another.

'You know I've got a few little mistresses who come up to see me, but I can always be honest with you about everything. There is only one Kate Kray and there always will be. That's the way I like it. *Nothing* can come between us – we'll stay married for good.

'You can have men friends too – of course you can – but you'll always be my wife.

'That's different.'

Yes, that's different.

## CHAPTER SEVEN

# *Hands Up*

Ron was not amused.

'You'll get me and Reggie a bad name,' he said.

'Hark at you,' I said. 'You're one of Britain's most notorious criminals!' He laughed – and then he gave me a real telling off.

Ron wasn't pleased when I got nicked for stealing £240 worth of stuff with a stolen credit card from Debenham's.

OK. Hands up. I was stupid. I hadn't done it before and there's no way I'd ever do it again. But I was skint and as I told Ron: 'It sounded so easy...'

He just looked at me as if I was off my rocker.

Yes, I suppose I must have been.

Before autumn 1992 I'd never been in trouble with the police, never been nicked for anything in my life. I've never been a thief. I don't steal things. But one day I was out with a friend of mine and it sounded like money for nothing. And it wasn't as if I'd be stealing from a person – if it was stealing it was stealing from a bank and it was just a little fraud, just a drop in the ocean as far as they were concerned...

We were sitting in a café having a coffee and I admired her jacket and asked her how much it cost.

'Nothing,' she said.

'What, you nicked it?'

'No, not exactly.'

Then she told me how she'd bought a credit card from some bloke and gone on a spending spree, bought loads of lovely clothes for herself, things for her house and even gone to Tesco's and done a big trolley-load of shopping. It sounded so easy.

When I saw Ron the next time I told him about it. At first he was mystified. I don't think they had credit cards when he was on the outside – at least not as many as there are now.

I said: 'You walk into the shop and get whatever you want and just give them the card. They give you a bit of paper and you sign it with the card and they look at it to see if the signatures match then they give you your card back and you just go. Then they send you a monthly statement and you pay so much a month.'

'What, don't you have to give them no money?'

'No,' I said. 'And, of course, if you've bought the card . . .'

'Don't do it,' he said. 'Don't do it. You shouldn't do that. You're a woman. Only men do things like that!'

I laughed at that. 'Oh come on, Ron. We had a woman Prime Minister for God knows how long.'

He had to agree with that. He and Reggie liked Margaret Thatcher. He thought she was strong and wouldn't be pushed around and Ron admired that in her. In fact, after she got sacked he and Reggie sent her a bouquet of flowers and a note saying they were sorry to hear that she was going.

But Ron thought the credit-card scam wasn't worth the bother. He knew I'd never been in trouble with the police and he certainly didn't want me to start now.

'Don't do it, Kate,' he said. I wish now I'd listened to him.

And I did forget about it for ages. Then months later, one Thursday night, Pa and I were out dancing at a night-club somewhere on the south coast. I was feeling happy – and a bit reckless. I went up to the bar and got chatting to a friend of mine and he offered to sell me a credit card. 'Fifty quid for this Diner's Card.'

'What the hell,' I thought and bought it.

The next morning I felt wrecked, but a friend of mine rang. She wanted me to go shopping with her because she was going on holiday the next day to Bognor Regis with her four kids. We wandered around the Lakeside shopping centre in West Thurrock and bought a few toys and books to keep the kids amused on the journey – shorts and t-shirts and things like that.

We ended up in Debenham's. The card was burning a hole in my pocket. Sue wanted four cushions for her sitting room, but she was skint too.

'Don't worry,' I said. 'I'll get them for you.'

I picked up the cushions and took them to the counter and gave the girl the card. She hardly looked at it. I was trying to look casual and confident, although inside I was suddenly nervous. What if the card wasn't OK? What if the machine didn't clear it?

But no problem. I signed, took my receipt and that was that.

'This is easy,' I thought.

Soon I was whizzing through the store having a whale of a time. More kiddies' clothes, a designer suit for me, some beautiful china plates for my flat, a cuddly toy for Sue's baby.

'I could get used to this,' I thought.

Sue needed some trainers for the kids.

'Let me,' I said. 'I'll get them – I'll treat the kids.' We laughed.

Deep inside Debenham's there was a sports shop, a franchise. Of course, being a novice at the credit-card scam, what I didn't realize was that that meant they had a different till and a different way of clearing the cards. I was feeling confident and cheerfully gave the girl my card. But while she was doing whatever she had to do the phone on her counter rang.

She picked it up and then she looked at me and in that instant I knew I'd been clocked. Shit!

'I'm just going to find my mate,' I said. But it was no good. The woman was on my case by then. I grabbed Sue, who was looking at some tracksuits.

'Just go! Quick!'

'What?'

'Go! GO!'

We took off through Debenham's with security guards in hot pursuit. The trouble was, we were in the middle of the store and couldn't find a way out and by now there were security guards on all the doors. I found out later that the professionals, the ones who are good at the credit-cards business, would never have got themselves into such a mess. You should always try the card out at a till by the door first so if anything goes wrong you can make a quick getaway. And, of course, you should be very wary of those franchise shops within a shop.

I found a door and made a dash for it. A man grabbed me.

'OK, OK, take your hands off me,' I said. 'I'm not going to make a fuss. Take your hands off me!'

They nicked Sue too.

'It's nothing to do with her,' I said. 'She's got four kids and she's going on holiday.'

That was the truth but of course they took no notice and unceremoniously we were carted off to the local nick where they separated us.

'How did you get here?' the policeman asked me.

'By bus,' I said, thinking of all the booty we'd bought and put in Sue's car.

'How did you get here?' they asked Sue in the next room.

'In my car,' she said, bless her. So we lost all the stuff we'd 'bought' and then the police ran a check on her car. She'd only just bought it through an ad in the local paper. It was second-hand, but it was in good condition. Now the police had to tell her she'd bought a ringer. So she lost the car as well! Poor Sue. It really wasn't her day.

They interviewed us together then and she was in floods of tears. She could have won an Oscar. 'My kids,' she cried. 'What about my kids? I've got to get home. I'm breastfeeding! And we're going to Bognor tomorrow!'

In the end it was pretty obvious even to the police that Sue didn't have a clue what was going on – and she'd just lost her car, too, so they let her go.

I felt resigned to the situation. Anyway, it was me who was guilty. And I'd been nicked. Hands up. Even so, I knew that Ron would be annoyed with me, so I didn't want them to find out that I was his wife.

I told the police my name was Kate Howard which, in

a way, is true because that was my name when I was married to Harry and it's still on some of my bank books and things like that.

They took all my belongings and put them in a plastic bag – and that's when they tumbled. I was a bit worried about giving them my things because of my jewellery – there was my wedding ring and the pinkie ring Ron had given me. I said to the policeman: 'That bag won't be opened again, will it? No one will touch my stuff? Give me your word.'

'Of course not,' he said. What I'd forgotten was that in my bag was a letter from Ron's friend Joey Pyle, who was then on remand. I can't remember what the letter was about – just the usual chatty things about how he was and how were me and Ron but, of course, it was addressed to Kate Kray.

By now I was feeling gutted. They put me in a stinky cell. My God, believe me, it's not very nice being locked up.

The walls were painted green. There were big heavy bars at the windows and there was a dirty, stinking toilet in a cubby hole in the corner. I was dying to go to the loo but there was no way I was going to go there.

I felt knackered after being out all night. I'd been silly. I'd been caught. I just wanted to get it all over with as soon as possible. I tried not to think about how I was going to explain it all to Ron. Most of all I tried to remember everything Ron said about being locked up. Ron told me that if it ever happened to me I'd hate it, and of course I did. Once they shut that door it was the pits.

Ron says that when you're first put in a cell you must

sleep. You mustn't let your thoughts take over. If you let those thoughts take over you'd go mad. I felt absolutely wrecked anyway, so I lay down on the little bed with its plastic cover, covered myself with the coarse blanket that was folded at the end of it and shut my eyes.

It wasn't long before they came to question me again.

'You're not Kate Howard, you're Kate Kray.'

He'd found Joey's letter – and the crafty gits had rung the prison where they were keeping Joey. 'Kate Kray – yeah, that's Ronnie's wife.'

'Got an address?'

'Yeah, she lives near Maidstone.'

I told the policeman that I'd never been arrested before in my life.

'I don't believe that,' he said. 'You've been asleep in this cell. I think you're a professional. Only a professional would be cool enough to do that.'

Well, that was a bloody joke. I felt like saying that if I was a professional, if I'd done this before, I wouldn't have been so careless as to get nicked in the first place!

'Where did you get the card?'

'I found it.'

'That's what they all say.'

'All right, I admit it. I bought it from a bloke in a club.'

'What's his name?'

'I don't know, how would I know? I just met him in the club and he offered to sell me the card and I bought it.'

They let me ring Harry to tell him what had happened and, as I was still there at eight o'clock at night, they allowed me to ring Broadmoor. I couldn't speak to Ron but at least I could send the message: 'Tell Ron I'll be up in the morning.'

The police assured me that it wouldn't get in the papers but I knew it would. All I was worried about was that I could get to Ron and explain what had happened before the papers did. The next morning I dashed up to Broadmoor.

'Ron, I've got to tell you, I was nicked yesterday. It's bound to get out and be in the papers.'

Ron was cross.

'It was terrible,' I said. 'They kept me in there for nine hours...'

'Nine hours!' he said. 'Nine hours! Hark at you! I've been inside for twenty-four years!' He laughed.

Then he told me off. I shouldn't be doing that kind of thing. I should have more sense. In the end, though, I think he did see a funny side. He kept winding me up, saying: 'Oh Kate, just think, you'll be put away with all those women and they'll all be after you.' He paused thoughtfully. 'Mind you, you'll probably be the tobacco baron within a week!'

He warned me that I wouldn't like being in the dock. He was right. I didn't. The court was the most scumbag court you've ever seen in your life, really rough, with all these winos outside lolling about. And there was Harry outside waiting for me. I was all dressed up and all the yobs kept coming up to me and saying: 'Are you my solicitor?'

The case was adjourned. Needless to say, when I came back for the proper hearing there were crowds of newspaper people and photographers all over the place. It was horrible. I hated it. I think more than anything else I was embarrassed – especially when they read out the list of what we'd got away with: cushions, plates, a dress, pairs of toddler's shorts and kiddies' books . . . I hated it.

'I knew you would,' said Ron.

I pleaded guilty – well, I was guilty, wasn't I? The prosecution wanted a custodial sentence – probably because my name is Kray – but fortunately the magistrates said that since it was my first offence they'd fine me instead – £240 plus £426 compensation. Over £600! That was one expensive shopping trip! Now you'll believe me when I say that I won't be trying that one again . . .

I didn't mind putting my hands up for the credit-card fraud. I did it. I was nicked fair and square. End of story. The only time I get annoyed is when they want you to put your hands up to something you didn't do.

I had the police on the doorstep after a ludicrous story appeared in the papers that Ron and I had bribed a couple of screws at Broadmoor. Absolute nonsense. The police went to see Ron and, not surprisingly, Ron would have none of it. So of course they came to see me.

I was at Harry's cottage when I looked out of the window and saw two men in plain clothes. I didn't know who they were, but my instinct was to go.

I was out of the back door like a shot! Harry answered the door.

'Is Mrs Kray in?' they said.

'No,' said Harry, and I wasn't. By then I was down the bottom of the garden trying to get out of the garden gate! The bloody thing wouldn't open so I climbed over it and I was shinnying up the wall when I looked up and there, at the end of the alleyway, were two other policemen just looking at me! I've never been so embarrassed in my life!

They came into the house.

'Did you bribe any of the nurses at Broadmoor?'

'No,' I said. I did admit that a couple of them had done driving jobs for me when I was running Silver Ladies, my Rolls-Royce chauffeur business, to earn a bit of extra money, but that was all. The men had been paid legitimately from the company's accounts and, as I pointed out: 'If I was going to bribe them why would I pay with Silver Ladies cheques? Look, here are the cheque stubs and here are the jobs they did – a couple of airport pick-ups . . .'

They questioned me again and again, but I kept telling them the truth and in the end they had to give up and go away. If I'd wanted to bribe the nurses I would have bribed them with cash. But why should I want to bribe them anyway? It was ridiculous.

After the credit-card business I didn't have any money. Mind you, before the credit-card business I was skint, which is why I suppose I did it in the first place. The chauffeur business was gone, so was the kissagram business. I didn't have any income – none at all, and I still had to pay my mortgage.

I've always worked, I've always kept myself. Even when I was married to Harry, he supported me, but I always paid my way.

I applied for various jobs. I liked the idea of being a croupier but as soon as any club found out who I was they wouldn't touch me with a barge-pole.

My friend Rosie came up with the idea of running a saucy chat line. She thought it would be easy money. She's a bit like me, always starting up different businesses – she used to run a postal gift company, sending out balloons in boxes and things like that.

She set up the phone business and asked if I'd like to have a go. So I went round there one day but I didn't like it. It made me feel uncomfortable. Some of these men are real pervs so I decided it wasn't for me.

But Rosie was coining it in. She had no intention of giving up. I'd pop around and see her every now and then and, although I didn't take the calls myself, I was there when the other girls did and sometimes it was a good laugh. Some of the calls were so funny.

The business worked like this. She advertised the number in the newspaper and then the men would ring up. They'd be told that they could pay by credit card or they could send a postal order and have their chat once the company had received it. Rosie had to have the money first. Most paid by credit card, so they could have their saucy chat there and then.

Their wives and girlfriends would never know, because she called the business 'Say It with Flowers' and that's how it came up on their credit-card statements!

All the girls adopted different names. They'd answer the phone and say, 'Thank you for calling. We charge five pounds for five minutes, ten pounds for ten minutes,' and so on.

The aim of the game was to get them off the phone – and get the money – as quickly as possible. And the secret was not to really listen to what they were saying. Some of the things were so disgusting. So for the sake of their own sanity the girls took little or no notice of what the man was saying.

They'd distract themselves with other things. Sometimes the girls would be watching 'Neighbours', or making a cup of tea or a sandwich, or doing the washing. They'd wander around with a portable phone clutched beneath one ear, absent-mindedly saying 'Ooh yes, that would be lovely!' and the man would rabbit on about whatever not knowing that in fact his chatline girl was really loading the washing machine!

One of the girls called herself Lena. She was a great laugh. She didn't have a very happy life. She was unhappily married and her husband could be a real pig. She hated him, but she couldn't bring herself to leave him.

She used to do nutty things to get her own back on him. Once she rolled his sausages in the cat litter before she grilled them for his supper! He said they were lovely spicy sausages . . . !

Another time she put two spoonfuls of Harpic in his take-away vindaloo. But that, she admitted, was going too far. He could have died and he was in agony for hours.

'We're not going to that curry house any more,' he said.

'No,' she said.

Lena told the men she was twenty-four years old, with long blonde hair and big boobs. In fact she's thirty-four with very short hair and virtually no boobs at all. She used to have me and Rosie in fits. She couldn't bring herself to say 'willy' or 'prick' or 'knob' – she thought it was far too rude and she just couldn't bring herself to say it. So instead we'd hear her make references to 'your hardness'.

'Do you want to put your hardness into my honeypot?' she would say while she was sitting there munching a cheese sandwich and watching the afternoon film. And

Rosie and I would be in the corner of the room literally screaming with laughter.

Then the man would say: 'Can I hear you do it to yourself?'

And we'd watch her pinch her cheek and then wiggle it about, going: 'Oooooh! Blllluuubbbbb, oooo! Bluuuuuubbbb! Thank you caller. Do ring again and ask for Lena. 'Bye!' And she'd carry on watching the telly!

She had one regular whose calls used to have us in hysterics. This man had a shoe shop nearby. He'd pay for half an hour and he'd say, 'I want you to pretend you've come into the shop to buy a pair of red stilettos.'

So Lena would put on a posh voice . . .

'Oh hello, I'd like to buy a pair of red stiletto shoes please . . .'

'Yes, madam. What size?'

'Oh, size five please . . . Ooh yes, what lovely shoes.'

'Do you want to try them on?'

'Yes please, can you just kneel at my feet and put the shoes on me. Don't they go well with my black stockings and suspenders . . .' (Much giggling in background from me and Rosie . . .)

'Yes, they're a lovely snug fit . . .'

'Would Madam like to walk around the shop to see if they fit properly . . .?'

'Oh yes, thank you. Yes, I shall walk up and down. Oh yes, they are lovely shoes.'

And then the man would say: 'Walk to the end of the shop and when you get to the end of the shop I'd like you to bend over the bargain bucket . . .!'

Lena was very good at the saucy chatlines and she was

also very funny. Once, Rosie picked up the phone and the man said: 'Can't I speak to anyone younger?' What a cheek!

So Lena went on the phone. 'Hello mister, that other lady said you wanted someone younger. I'm eighteen.'

All he wanted her to do was to smoke a cigarette over the phone. You'd be surprised how many men rang up and asked for that. Very odd, Lena said.

A lot of them wanted to hear the girl do a wee, so Rosie kept a glass and a jug of water by the phone so the girl just poured the water into the jug. It was mental!

Lena was also a bit naïve. When one man asked her if she did water sports, she said: 'Well I went water skiing once!' And when another asked her what she'd do with his dog she said, 'Take it for a walk?!'

But Rosie drew the line at any chat about animals or children. That was a firm rule.

We had a good laugh, but I didn't want to get into that kind of business and they went bust anyway when the credit-card companies found out what Say It with Flowers really was!

If I had the choice, I'd probably still be running the kissagram business. But after being set up and appearing in the paper I can't do that any more. It was hard work but we had such fun. I called it Kandy's after the song 'Your kiss is sweet, as sweet as Kandy...'

Some of the things people asked for were really mental. Sometimes I'd be asked to dress up as a Salvation Army woman. The people would brief me beforehand, saying: 'Birthday Boy will be wearing a red jumper and sitting in the corner.' Then I'd go around the pub shaking my tin and saying, 'Halleluyah, brother' until I got to him. People used to put money in the tin, but I always gave it to the bloke behind the bar for the collection box.

Sometimes I'd do a double act with my mate Angie, who's as nutty as a fruitcake. A great girl. She was my roly-polygram girl. Angie won't mind me saying so, but she is massive. I mean mega-massive. She is really as big as a pudding. For one kissagram I actually made her dress up as a giant Christmas pudding.

She was a great success. I had made the brown and black outfit with big hoops underneath to hold the dress out and I stuck a bit of holly on her head. I went to collect her for the job and I just collapsed with laughter. There she was, a great big Christmas pudding with the holly on her head, standing on the doorstep saying: 'Kate, I can't do this. Kate, I'm not going to this. Kate, don't make me do this.' But she did, good old Angie.

Another time she was hired by some farm boys locally. She was dressed up as a giant parrot, put on a tractor and dragged out into the middle of a field of lettuces to sing her birthday song to one of the lads who was working there.

At stag nights we'd go along together – me as a heavily pregnant bride in the long white dress and Angie as the irate mother-in-law with rollers in her hair. She looked just like Les Dawson. Then she'd say to the bridegroom: 'Look, what have you done to my daughter!' and bash him with her handbag!

We spent a lot of time laughing. She was with me once when I had to do a Salvation Army-gram for some bloke who worked in a car-repair garage. I drove in and wound down the window and said to the garage mechanics: 'Brothers, it's broke!' They loved it! I got out of the car, did the job and looked round. All you could see was my Volkswagen Beetle swaying from side to side. It was Angie inside laughing.

The whipping job she did for me was mad. She had to do a roly-polygram for a builder at a working man's cafe at eight in the morning.

'What have I got to do, then?' said Ange, all dressed up in her sexy roly-poly gear. I gave her a whip.

'Well,' I said. 'You go in there and get a sausage off his plate and stick it in his mouth. Then you make him kneel down and you get out your whip and whip the sausage out of his mouth.'

'All right,' she said. 'But don't come in with me 'cause you'll make me laugh.'

So I stood outside with my nose pressed against the window. It was chaos. She missed the sausage and got the man down the side of the face! Then she managed to get the sausage and I was shouting through the window: 'Get the egg! Get the egg!' The men were falling about, but I don't know if their victim enjoyed it very much. Angie overwhelmed him and she didn't do too many whipping ones after that.

Her forte was the balloonagram. She blew up lots of balloons and attached them to a big belt. Then when she burst in on the birthday party she undid the man's flies and attached a Kandygram badge to his trousers with the pin facing outwards. Next he had to thrust his loins until he burst all her balloons. It was mad, really mad.

I tell Ron these stories and he says: 'They're madder out there than they are in here!'

One thing I discovered when I was doing the kissagrams is that people don't always give them as a present because they like you – sometimes they give them because they can't bloody stand you!

I was once hired by some junior doctors to do an Easter Bunny-gram at Pembury hospital for their consultant. I had to dress up as a rabbit with big pink ears and a pink basque and stockings and suspenders. When I arrived they said: 'We're going to put you in this bed with the covers up to your neck and draw the curtains around you. You'll hear us doing the rounds, so just wait until we get to your bed and we draw back the curtains.'

So I lay there in the geriatric ward, dressed as a rabbit, and suddenly I heard one of the doctors say to someone: 'This lady has just been brought in – she's got something wrong with her eyes . . .' Myxomatosis, I suppose.

The curtains were drawn back. And there was the consultant in his pin-striped suit. I hopped out of bed and started singing: 'I'm your Easter Bunny . . .' and the students were falling about with laughter. He was in total shock. There was me thinking they'd done it because they liked him – they didn't, they did it because they thought he was a right git!

He was furious. He went striding out of the curtains and down the ward with me hopping after him singing 'I'm your Easter bunny . . .' and all those poor old people were sitting in the chairs next to their beds absolutely rigid and wondering 'Was that a rabbit?!'

The next time I was an Easter Bunny was when a class

of schoolkids ordered a Bunny-gram for their schoolmaster. Again I thought it was because they thought he was a nice teacher. They didn't, they thought he was a right sod! They clubbed together to pay for it and told me to turn up and wait outside the classroom until they banged the door. Then I was to burst in and sing: 'I'm your Easter Bunny...'

So that's what I did and the teacher went berserk! He was livid. He didn't think it was funny at all.

'Get out! Get out!' he screamed. 'You're trespassing, get off these premises!'

'I can't be trespassing,' I said. 'I'm a rabbit! I'm a free-spirited bunny.' Hop, hop, hop.

The kids, of course, loved every minute of it. Suddenly all their desks flew up and they all brought out cameras and they were falling around with laughter. But the teacher was a miserable old git and he ordered me to leave the school.

Nutty things, we did. Every day was different – one day I was a French maid, the next a nun, the next a belly dancer. I do miss it. But after I married Ron it all changed. Ron warned me I'd be set up, and I was, and then even the ordinary ones turned a bit sour. Some people were amazing. I went to one party and Birthday Boy was horrified. He kept shrieking: 'Get away from me! I know who you're married to! I'm not having my picture taken with you! Go away!'

I said: 'It will be all right, don't be silly.' But he was serious. It spoilt the whole thing. It wasn't fun any more.

Now I'm looking for another job – more than that, a

career. I've started an intensive computer course at the local college. Just about every job these days involves computers in some way so it's bound to prove useful.

But I'm undecided about what kind of career to follow. I don't know. However, I can tell you one thing: it will be strictly legal and legit. I've learned my lesson on that one and I don't ever intend being locked up again.

## CHAPTER EIGHT

# *Friend or Foe?*

It was early in June when the phone rang. It was Broadmoor. And it was bad news. There had been an incident, they said. Ron had tried to strangle another man on his ward.

I couldn't believe it. In fifteen years Ron has never been in trouble because of violence. He's never been involved in any fights, nothing. As one of the screws once said to me: 'Ron would rather give someone a packet of fags and walk away than get involved in a fight.'

Ron's doctor came on the phone to talk to me.

'His mental health has deteriorated badly,' he said. 'He's very poorly, feeling very paranoid. You won't be able to visit him in the main hall. We don't want him under any pressure.

'We've moved him to Abingdon Ward for a while.'

Abingdon Ward is like an intensive-care ward where patients get one-to-one nursing. It's where they're taken when they're badly into their mental illness.

I'm still not entirely sure what happened that Monday lunchtime in Broadmoor. Ron doesn't like talking about it, although he did tell me that it was his fault and no fault of the other man.

They were all in the dining room having lunch and something sparked Ron off. He got hold of a man called Lee Kiernender, a big bloke in his early thirties. I don't know Kierneneder, although Ron did once ask me to buy him a new pair of trainers.

Ron got Kiernender in an arm lock and it took several nurses to pull him off. Kiernender passed out and was taken to intensive care. He was turning blue and close to death, the papers said.

'But Ron can't have wanted to kill him,' Reggie told me. 'Ron and I were taught that arm lock many years ago. One jerk of the arm and you make a man unconscious. Two and you can easily break his neck. Ron didn't do that.'

Two days later the story was in the newspapers, but the reasons the papers gave for Ron attacking the man were rubbish. One said that Ron objected to Kiernender because he was happy and singing.

That's not true. Ron likes happy people – it's the ones who are always moaning that he can't stand.

Another newspaper said it was because of what the man had done outside. Again, not true. If Ron got into fights with patients in Broadmoor because of what they'd done on the outside he'd be getting into fights every day of the week. And he hasn't had a fight in fifteen years.

But Ron wasn't feeling well. That was obvious when they let me see him on Abingdon a couple of days later. I was a bit apprehensive about the visit. I'd never been on a ward before, especially a ward like Abingdon. I had a picture in my mind of a grim, dark punishment block in the old part of the hospital with bars everywhere.

But it was nothing like that. Abingdon is in the wing Princess Diana opened a couple of years ago. It's very modern, light and spacious and furnished in pale colours like lemon and sky-blue. The day room, where I was to meet Ron, is like a modern reception area, carpeted, with easy chairs and a hot-drinks machine and, from the window, the patients look out on to a big fish pond full of Koi carp.

There are, understandably, a lot of nurses about and the atmosphere is very calm and quiet.

They brought Ron to see me and he looked OK, but his face was pale and he'd obviously lost a lot of weight. I wasn't going to have a go at him. I am his wife and he was obviously poorly. We both knew what had happened was serious but I tried to take the dairy off of it – to lighten things a little.

So I smiled and said: 'You've been a little bugger, haven't you?'

We sat talking for half an hour while two screws sat not very far away. He was pleased to see me. We're not the kind of people who throw their arms around each other saying: 'I love you! I love you!' But we sat together and I rubbed his back for him.

'I'd understand if you wouldn't want to be with me any more,' said Ron, 'because after this I'm never coming out of here.'

'Well,' I said, 'I've never known you out anyway so it's no difference to me. Anyway, you will come out one day if I have to push you out in a bloody bath chair!'

'You're a loyal girl,' he said.

I didn't stay long. Ron didn't want to talk about what had happened, apart from to say it was his fault, and I didn't want to ask. The other man, I later found out, is fine and fully recovered, thank goodness.

As I write this Ron has been on Abingdon Ward for some weeks and hopes to be moved back to his old room on Henley Ward. Each time I see him he's a little better.

'I'd understand if you divorced me,' he says. I make a joke of it.

'What do I want to be divorced from you for? I can have sex outside, I can have relationships and you don't mind. What do I want a divorce for?'

I've got to know many of the nurses at Broadmoor over the years and after the incident with Kiernender a lot of them kept coming up to me.

'How is he, Kate?' they said. 'Why did it happen? What's come over Ron? We couldn't believe it. He's never been any trouble.'

I believe I know why and I think the people closest to Ron know why. He was very upset in the weeks before it happened and that made him ill. And the person who upset him was his own brother Charlie.

You may be surprised to see that there are no pictures of Charlie in this book. That's deliberate. Ron won't have it.

Many people believe that Charlie doesn't really want the twins to come out because it's not in his best interests if they do. While they're away he's number one. He can swan about being *the* Kray.

When they were out he was always in second place. And when they come out again he'll be in second place again.

I knew – and Charlie knew – that Ron hadn't been feeling well for a while before the Kiernender incident.

Then, suddenly, Ronnie and Reggie discovered that

Charlie had written another book, *We Did the Business*, with author Colin Fry, and it was going to be serialized in a Sunday newspaper. They were shocked.

He hadn't even had the courtesy or the respect to tell them that he was doing it. Ronnie only knew because one of the twins' journalist friends had rung and told them that it was going in the paper that Sunday.

Well, some people might say, why should Charlie tell them? Why? Because it was about them. Ron and Reg are quite used to people like Lambrianou writing books about them without saying a word about it, but they didn't expect that from their own brother.

That was bad enough. Then they read what he had written and they were both very upset. Most of the book was about Ron, and Charlie had written, among other things, that when Ron went to America he was intimidated by the Mafia bosses and was frightened for the first time in his life.

It was untrue, and after that was printed I was bombarded with calls from Ron's friends – and some of his former enemies too – who kept saying: 'What the fuck's Charlie on about? Everybody knows these stories aren't right. Ronnie was one of the most fearless men in London.'

No one could believe that Charlie had been so disrespectful and so disloyal to his own brother.

Over the years Ronnie and Reggie have taken all the lies and the crap that's been written about them, and they've been betrayed by people who they considered to be friends, but this betrayal was different. This was their own brother.

In their own books they've hardly mentioned Charlie – and they certainly would never mug him off.

They were both shocked and very upset. Reggie was upset at the way Charlie portrayed Ronnie and, for Ronnie, I think it was a turning point. He wasn't feeling well and he was so upset by it that in my opinion it just tipped the scales. The Kiernender incident happened shortly afterwards.

In the six years I've known the twins Charlie has only been to see them a few times. Ron feels that Charlie could have been more of a brother to him and Reggie.

I have always thought that if anyone had the right to speak about Ron and Reg it's got to be Charlie, because he's their elder brother and he's known them all their lives, and I will say that until this summer I've always had the greatest respect for him.

When there have been rows between Ron and Reg and Charlie, I've never taken sides because I've never seen it as my place to interfere – after all, after six years I'm a relative newcomer to the Kray family. And I feel apprehensive about speaking out like this but this time I can't keep schtum. I think the twins have got the right to say for the first time how they really feel about Charlie: angry and badly let down.

Charlie kept very quiet about what he was up to and, with hindsight, we should have suspected something. For quite a while none of our friends saw him and his phone was cut off.

He'd gone underground. As I write this he still is, and I'm not surprised. He knew full well what the effect would be on Ron when he read crap like that.

'I never want to see Charlie again and I'll never forgive him,' Ron told me. And the saddest thing of all was what he said next. 'He's no longer my brother. I don't have two brothers any more. Just Reggie.'

And he means it too.

Ron says: 'If you want a friend – be a friend.'

I think Ron is a good friend. He's certainly been a good friend to me, as well as a caring husband. I can confide in Ron and the person I go to for advice is Ron. I don't always take it! But I *do* listen. I can talk to Ron about anything, anything in the world.

He's not a selfish man – he genuinely wants me to be happy and get on with making the most out of life. He's incredibly supportive, especially about things like my computer course at the local college.

'I want to do it – but I don't know if I can. I'm not very clever,' I said.

'Rubbish,' says Ron. 'You want to do it, so do it.'

I think Ron is good to his friends, too. If they're in trouble they can go to Ron and he helps them as much as he can. It's not just a case of helping them out with a bit of cash occasionally. He'll support them. And if they think a letter or a phonecall from Ron will help matters, he'll do it. He doesn't let people down.

I think it's because he's such a good friend that he makes such a formidable enemy. Ron is incredibly loyal to his friends – Reg too – so he automatically expects other people to be the same.

And that, of course, isn't always the case.

Ron remembers the old days of the Firm as if they were yesterday. To a certain extent he and Reg live on their memories – they have to. Those are their only memories of the outside, so they keep them fresh and alive more than perhaps we, who have twenty-five more years of memories of ordinary life, do.

Ron cannot forget the so-called 'friends' who betrayed the twins back in the 1960s. And he cannot forgive them.

I asked him once if he still felt bitter towards them after all this time. The reply was instant.

'Bitter?' he said. 'Yes, I'm bitter towards them. I'll never forgive them. Never. They came to our house. My mother used to feed them and Reggie and I looked after them. They're nothing but slags and I will never forgive them.'

Ask who 'they' are, and Ron reels off the list without hesitation: 'Bill Ackerman, Albert Donaghue, the Barry Brothers, Ronnie Hart . . .'

What Ron says about Bill Ackerman is unrepeatable here. He says that Ackerman was never a member of the Firm, despite his claims to the contrary, and Ron claims that Ackerman is always full of stories about the twins because he wants to make sure they never come out. 'He's a slag and a rat and he lives in Eastbourne!' I won't go on – it's not a lady's place to slag men off.

Albert Donaghue was a member of the Firm who admitted being involved in the abduction of Frank Mitchell, 'the Mad Axeman' from Dartmoor prison. Ron and Reg were tried for Mitchell's murder and acquitted – but during the trial Donaghue turned Queen's evidence and made many allegations against the twins which they strenuously, and successfully, denied.

Brothers John and Tony Barry used to run the Regency

Club in London after Ron and Reg gave it up. Tony Barry was a co-defendent at the Old Bailey trial when the twins were accused of murdering George Cornell and Jack McVitie.

Ronnie Hart, a young cousin of the twins, was present when Jack McVitie was killed. He gave evidence against the twins during their trial.

And there are others who Ron has no time for. There's Tony Lambrianou – a member of the Firm – who appeared in the dock with them during their trial.

'A — grass' Ron's opinion of him. At least, that's the only thing I can write here!

Mention the name of his cousin Johnny Kray to Ron and his face changes. Johnny runs a pub in Kent.

'Johnny is not family.' Ron said: 'He never lifted a finger to help our mother when Reg and I were sent away. He could have helped her.

'Maybe our name has helped him in his business, but in twenty-five years he's never once been to visit either of us. He's never even sent a Christmas card – never even a packet of fags.'

And, of course, there's one other name on Ron's list of people we don't want to know: Gillett. I am a forgiving person. I find it easier to forgive than Ron – but then I haven't been banged up in prison for twenty-five years. But even I don't forgive Gillett.

Ron hates disloyalty, he hates lies, he hates grasses. He and Reg would rather die than grass. If they had grassed on other people they probably would have been out long since.

But there are some other people who make me bloody

mad – because of the way they've taken advantage of Ron and Reg.

The Krays have become almost legendary figures. Twenty-five years on and people are still fascinated by them. And where there is fascination there is money to be made – and many people have made money out of Ron and Reg.

All those books. Ron doesn't mind people writing about the twins. 'Good luck to them,' he says, 'if they can make a few bob.'

But *I* think it's a diabolical liberty that people write about the twins – not just their crimes, but about their early life and their supposed emotions and behaviour. They put a photo of the twins on the cover of their books because they know that way they'll sell more and make more money, and then don't even have the courtesy to contact Ron or Reg or ask them if they mind. They give them no thanks and no money. I just think it's a bloody nerve. All those people making money out of their name.

Ron and Reg are doing their time. They've been locked away for twenty-five years. It is their story, their lives – if anyone's going to make money out of it, it should be them. Ron doesn't get as annoyed about it as I do. He would just appreciate the occasional gesture – a packet of fags, a 'thanks, Ron'.

Did Tony Lambrianou give them any money from his best-selling book? No. Nipper Read, too – he put them on his cover. No.

If people were writing about you and they made bundles of money out of you and didn't give you so much as a thank-you, wouldn't you think that was a bit of a liberty? Of course you would.

'Bloody cheek!' I say to Ron.

He smiles. He's used to it.

I wouldn't mind so much if all the stories were true. But some of them seem to get wilder as the years pass by. Ron says that some people make up stories because they want to make sure than he and Reg never get out.

Ron is philosophical. He'll come out when the doctors say he's well enough. But it's all so unfair on Reggie. How many other people have been sent down for one murder and are still banged up after twenty-five years? I'm not saying that what he did was right. But how many?

I think the crux of the matter is that no Home Secretary has the nerve to be the man who let the Krays out. It's all political.

So, there are enemies, yes. But there are friends too. Ron and Reg have many, many brilliant friends who have stuck by them, who've encouraged them, given them strength.

There are some Ron particularly wants me to mention – and there are people he wants to remember in this book.

Ron says that the man he most respected years ago was called Billy Bligh. It was Billy Bligh's niece, Monica, who Ron was going out with when he was sent away.

In his new book, *Villains We Have Known*, Reggie writes about Billy Bligh. This is how he describes him:

> Billy, a total villain, hailed from Clerkenwell in North London... Ron and I spent time with him on remand in Brixton prison and saw him

regularly at racetracks all over the country. He was a smaller man than Jimmy Essex with a bald head, high cheekbones and hollowed cheeks caused by the ulcers from which he suffered.

His eyes were inertly blue and through their intensity one could perceive he was a man who did not tolerate fools. With his gaunt frail appearance, one could easily misjudge his personality, for concealed beneath the superficial exterior was one of the most ruthless villains ever to be born in London.

The other man Ron wants to remember is Lesley Burnham, a good friend, and Charlie Clark who they called the 'Cat Man' – not because he was a good cat burglar – which he was! – but because he loved cats! I met him only once. He hadn't seen Ron for twenty years and Ron asked me to pick him up from the station closest to Broadmoor.

He wasn't hard to recognize. There he was, all suit to boot, an overcoat draped over his shoulders. What Ron didn't tell me was that he had a false leg. As we walked across Broadmoor's courtyard on our way to see Ronnie I suddenly heard a clatter behind me.

I looked around and there was the Cat Man hopping about. I picked up his leg – 'I take it that's yours?' – then we walked in to see Ron, me holding the Cat Man up with one arm and carrying his lost leg under the other. Ron roared with laughter when he saw us and they had a very good visit.

Afterwards the Cat Man was in tears, and said it was

the best day he'd had in years, seeing Ronnie again. I was glad because sadly the old boy was murdered a few months later by a boy who broke into his home.

Ron would like me to mention Joey Pagano, a businessman from New York. He met him there in the 1960s and they became good friends. Joey was reputed to be a Mafia boss.

Over the pond they called him the 'Man Amongst Men'. He, like Ron, was a very generous man. He never forgot his humble origins and always looked after his friends. A few years ago he sent Ron a lovely 'pinkie' ring of gold and diamonds which Ron still wears today.

Ron was very upset when Joey died recently. They'd kept in touch regularly and exchanged cards and letters for a long time. Ron wrote a poem dedicated to Joey which he sent to his family as a tribute.

Some of the friends Ron feels deserve a special mention, like Joey, I don't know for obvious reasons.

There's Bill Gentry, who bought El Morocco Club in Gerrard Street, Soho, from Ron and Reg; Ron Easterbrook, Joey Martin – all lifers; Tony Burns, who runs the Repton Boxing Club in East London and Johnny Nash, a London businessman, who the twins have known since they were picked up on the run from the Army and put in Shepton Mallet prison when they were just sixteen.

There's Bill Curbishley who runs a record company and Billy Murray, who looks like a villain, talks like a villain but is, in fact, a very successful actor who's appeared in TV's 'London's Burning', 'Bergerac' and 'EastEnders'. He loves Ron and phones every three months or so to see if there's anything he needs. A very nice man.

And I mustn't forget our wedding guests – Alec Steen, Wilf Pine and Joey Pyle. Joey, described recently by the newspapers as 'one of Britain's top gangsters . . . who had run a worldwide organization, which extended as far as connections with the Mafia', is now serving fourteen years in prison.

Ron and Reg know him differently. In his *Villains* book Reggie wrote:

> During the 1950s and 1960s, if one went to the Astor Club, just off Berkeley Square, or to the Pigalle Restaurant in Regent Street, in the early hours of the morning, one would be sure to meet up with Joe Pyle who came from Morden in Surrey.
>
> Joe has always been an easygoing, likeable person, and at times his good looks could deceive, because in his twenties he had been a good middleweight professional fighter. Joe has always been a good businessman and a man of his word.
>
> During the 1960s he had been acquitted of murder during the Pen Club case when Jimmy Nash had been found guilty of manslaughter and sentenced to five years in prison. Joe used to come to the East End regularly to have a drink with us and we, in turn, would go to the West End to see Joe, to return the compliment. He used to have his monogram on the left-hand side of the chest of his shirts, which were always beautiful linen.
>
> Joe is a loyal friend.

That's true. For years Joey has visited Ron and Reg. He was there the first time I met Ron and I've always liked him, which is why I went to a party for him earlier this year in a pub in Morden, his manor, where his friends and family got together to try and raise some money for his appeal.

Ron, Reg and many of his friends were very sad the day Joey was sent down. He's fifty-six years old now – and we hope he's successful with his appeal.

All these are good friends of Ron's and there are more, too many to mention here.

When it comes to his friends and family, Ron is very soft-hearted but, as he says, 'Only a fool takes kindness as weakness.' Ron is also amazingly psychic. It's not just his psychic link with Reggie. He's also psychic about what's going to happen to his friends. He 'sees' things before they happen, and he 'knows' things.

It was like the time I saw him before I was rushed to hospital. We had a normal visit and it was on the drive back that I started to get these pains in my stomach. When I got home the phone was ringing and it was Broadmoor. They said: 'Ron's worried about you – he says you're in pain. Are you all right?'

I swear that I never said a single word about feeling ill when I was with Ron – I didn't feel ill then and I looked fine. He says that after I left he just 'knew' I was ill and had pains in my stomach.

If Ron puts a curse on anyone it always comes true. He put a curse on the judge who sent him away, Melford Stevenson, and I think it all came true. He said he'd go blind, get cancer and die – and he did. Reggie didn't want him to tell anyone about the curse but Ron was adamant. And he put a curse on that bastard Gillett after that story about me appeared in the newspapers. He said his hair would fall out, his wife would leave him, he'd lose his house and he'd end up in the nick. It all came true.

Sometimes during a visit he'll say: 'Last night something came to me . . . this is going to happen . . .' and nine times out of ten it does happen.

Once I went to see him and he said: 'Last night I had this terrible dream about you having a smashed-up face. It kept coming to me.'

'Oh get away, I'm fine.'

But two days later I had a crash in my BMW and ended up on the lawn of the local bowling club. I broke my nose and I had two big black eyes. I went to see Ron and he went mad. I said I'd had an accident.

'You didn't have an accident. Someone's beaten you up! Who's done this to you? Tell me, who's done this to you?'

'It's you, you sod,' I said. 'You did it! You told me it would happen and it did!'

Ron believes in God and he also believes in an afterlife. He believes that people who have loved us look after us from the other side and are often very close. Every night, without fail, he says that just as he's falling asleep he feels a hand press down on his left shoulder. It's not always at the same time, but it's always at night and always just as he's dropping off to sleep.

Ron doesn't know who it is; maybe it's his mother Violet. But he says it doesn't frighten him – just the opposite. He says it's comforting and reassuring. The hand of a friend. But the experience of feeling an invisible hand on the shoulder is apparently common among psychics and many of the top psychic healers say they feel just the same when they are healing someone.

Friendship in one way or another is what has kept Ron and Reg going over the years, and they do have many brilliant friends. But there are also the people who like to pretend that they're friends. They give me the needle. So many people want to be associated with the Krays and so many people want other people to know that they know the Krays.

Maybe they met Ron or Reg once – some of them never met them at all – but they'll come up to me and say: 'Give my regards to the Colonel.' I'll tell Ron and he hasn't a clue who they are. They boast about how friendly they are with the Krays. But of these same people not one of them go and visit the twins, or send them some tobacco or bring them any business.

A lot of men who've been in prison claim to have met the Krays there and become friends. Well, maybe they did meet Ron or Reg but that doesn't necessarily mean they're friends.

Ron says that being in prison is like being in the outside world in a way – you don't expect to like and respect everyone you meet, do you? Just because Ron and Reg have been inside for so long doesn't make them any different, they don't automatically like and respect all the other inmates. Some of the people they've met – the child molesters and the rapists – they despise.

Ron says that some of the people he's met inside have been real slags. 'They've got no moral standards,' he says.

As well as friends, there are the Kray fans, some of them famous.

Ron and Reg knew many of the big names of their day. Some, like Diana Dors and Barbara Windsor, became good and close friends. Diana, Ron says, was a lovely woman. She used to visit Ron's mum after the twins were put away and they appreciated that. When she died of cancer and then Alan Lake, her husband, committed suicide, Ron was upset. It was such a shame.

The singer David Essex is another old acquaintance. The twins gave him a singing break in their club, El Morocco. Stars of today, who are too young to remember when the Krays were out, are fascinated by them just the same.

Jon Bon Jovi's been up to see Ron, as has Jimmy White, the snooker player. The Kemp twins, Gary and Martin, also visited Ron when they were making the film, *The Krays*.

The actor Charlton Heston was in the public gallery of the Old Bailey for part of the twins' trial and he hasn't forgotten Ron. And the blonde American star Debbie Harry has written to him.

The one star Ron would have liked to have met at one time was Kylie Minogue, who he thought was lovely. He likes 'Neighbours'.

And, of course, there are the real Kray fans, ordinary people who've never met Ron or Reg but who just love them. Some of them are really nutty, but most of them are very sweet.

I get to meet them quite regularly at the parties they put on every now and then. Hundreds of people turn up and, whatever you think about the Krays, you must admit that the twins are pretty extraordinary to have so many fans after they've been away for so many years.

The party I went to in March 1993 was pretty typical – there were over three hundred people there and they made quite an evening of it. There was a buffet, a disco and live band and they were selling Kray t-shirts, books and baseball caps.

The organizers were worried I'd be mobbed, so they got me a couple of minders and they sent a limo to collect me and my friend Flanagan, who was coming with me. I met Flanagan on my wedding night at the party we had at the Hilton. She's a lovely girl, great fun.

She's been around Ron and Reg for years and she was one of the first ever Page Three girls. There is no way to explain Flanagan; she is like a whirlwind! She's now fifty, but she is still as vivacious as a teenager. She's got a heart of gold and she's very, very fiery – as many of her boy-friends would confirm!

Flanagan and I sat in the back of the limo driving up to London, her in her mink and me in my fox-fur coat, both feeling good. The driver wouldn't even let us open the car door for ourselves. It was just like the film *The Bodyguard*!

When we got there everyone tried to crowd around me – it was as if the Queen Mother had arrived and some of them were kissing my hand. You should have seen it, I was terribly embarrassed! The minders led us to our table. The whole thing was amazing.

In fact, the minders were a bit over-protective. I don't think any of the Kray fans would hurt me. One of the fans came up and said: 'Would you sign my autograph book for me?' But before he could get anywhere near me, the minders had blocked his way.

'Go on, I don't mind,' I said. And soon there were queues of them. One was a very nice man called John Griffiths who's been a fan of the Krays for ages and who Ron regards as a special friend. Every week he sends Ron little parcels, sometimes cigarettes or books or Ron's favourite boxing magazines. Ron had told me about him.

John was very disappointed.

'I wrote to Ron,' he told me, 'and Ron said he'd like to see a photo of me. I wanted to get a photo of you and me together but they've confiscated my camera.'

I found out that for some reason they'd confiscated all the cameras. So I said: 'You go and get your camera and you come and have your picture done.'

'I can't allow that,' said the minder.

'Look,' I said, 'all these people have made an effort to come here. They're buying books, they're supporting Ron and Reg...' So in the end I had my photo taken with hundreds of them!

You meet all sorts at these parties. There was one bloke there who'd changed his name by deed poll to Ronnie Kray – I nearly fainted when he said: 'Hello, I'm Ronnie Kray!' And then there was the bloke who wanted me to autograph his shoulder. Then he was going straight off to have it tattooed on!

A few days after the party, I went to see Ron as usual and he was feeling really good. He'd had dozens of cards from people who'd been at the party, all saying how good it was and how much they'd enjoyed themselves.

'They said you were really nice to them,' he said, 'and I should be proud of you. Well, I am proud of you, you know that, Kate.'

Sometimes friends of the Krays organize parties to raise money for charity. One was a very flashy boxing do which they'd put on to raise money for a little boy who was dying. Everyone enjoyed a three-course dinner and then watched a boxing competition in a ring in the centre of the restaurant. They got young boxers to compete and I was to give out the cups and trophies. There were all these elegant people there, it really was a star-studded audience.

Suddenly the compère said over the microphone: 'Can I have some quiet please. Reggie Kray is calling us from Lewes prison . . .'

And then there was Reggie's voice booming out around the hall: 'Hello, Reggie Kray here! Thank you all for coming. Hope you have a good time and raise lots of money for the little boy . . .' but then he carried on. I don't think he realized he was being broadcast to hundreds of people. Well, why should he? He's been inside for twenty-five years and he couldn't see the hall and all the people.

So he went on 'Got any news? Got any messages? And can you tell so and so . . .'

We did laugh! It was very funny, and Reggie and Ronnie saw the funny side of it too.

The twins have always had their fans. In the old days all kinds of celebrities used to come to their clubs. When Ron was in the dock he told the court: 'If I wasn't here now I'd probably be having a drink with Judy Garland!' And that was probably true!

Sometimes when I see Ron I'll mention a famous name from the 1960s, just in conversation, an actor or a singer, and he says in a matter-of-fact but never boastful way: 'Oh her – yes, I knew her.'

Why were all these people attracted to the Krays? I think it was because they've always had and still have an aura about them. And, no doubt, the celebrities thought they were living a bit dangerously, mixing with gangsters in a Kray club. But there was never any trouble there. They were as safe as houses!

Ron and Reg have always had friends from the aristocracy, too. My favourite was a real lady who I'll call Lady Jane. I think they met her through a friend, and she used to visit them. She was a very elegant lady, about fifty, and she always wore nice jewellery. She had business interests in South Africa and she went to Ron for advice with some deal or other. She spoke with a very posh accent – and she was terribly funny, although often unintentionally so.

She'd ring Broadmoor and say: 'This is Lady Jane and I'd like to come and see Mr Kray.' Ron said that when she visited him it was the only time he'd ever seen flowers on the table in the visiting hall!

She was very naïve. She rang the prison where they were keeping Reggie at the time, and said: 'This is Lady Jane . . . Please can I speak to Mr Reggie Kray?!'

'No,' they said.

'But I am Lady Jane . . .' she said.

And they said: 'We don't care who you are, no, you can't speak to him!'

Lady Jane was absolutely amazed. She couldn't understand it at all.

onnie and I had our marriage blessed in the chapel at
roadmoor. It was a simple service but very nice, although
on was a bit annoyed that the hospital wouldn't allow all
ur guests to attend.

*Above:* Cheers! At the wedding we were allowed to serve champagne. Needless to say, Ron enjoyed his first drink in a very long time. He was only supposed to have one glass but his friends kept topping it up!

*Opposite top*: Man and wife – it's official! Ron hates having his photo taken and getting him to smile for the camera was a bit of problem until his friend, Joey Pyle, came to the rescue and joke "Oi, Ron, Nipper Read's dead!" Laughs all round!

*Opposite below:* After the wedding in Broadmoor we gave a big party at the Bracknell Hilton. Here's two of Ronnie's closest friends tucking into the buffet – Ronnie Fields on the left and Joey Pyle on the right. You can see the back of my wedding dres and there's another friend, Alec Steen, on the left wearing his dark glasses. He never takes them off – even for weddings !

*Top:* Another party night – this one to raise money for Joey Pyle appeal. He was sent away at Christmas for involvement in a drug smuggling operation. This is me and our friend, the unlicensed boxing champion, Lenny McLean.

*Above:* Same party – me, Alec, the famous Flanagan, Davey Lar and, on the left, a friend.

ɔok happy enough but this was taken at a party when I was
ɩt recovering from my nervous breakdown. That's why my
ɩr is so short – when I was ill, on impulse, I had it all chopped
and dyed white! With me are Flanagan, on the right, and
ge Three girl, Tracy Elvick.

*Top*: This is my favourite picture of Harry, my ex-husband and, apart from Ron, my closest friend.

*Above left:* This is Mohammed Kamhmer, a fellow patient and c of Ronnie's friends in Broadmoor. A very nice bloke.

*Above right:* I think Reggie looks really dishy in this picture. I always tease him that he looked like Richard Gere in those days

*p right:* Ronnie's favourite picture of me which was taken by rd Lichfield. Ronnie keeps this on the wall of his room in ɔadmoor.

*ove:* Before Ron and I married I used to run Silver Ladies, a ıffeur car business. Here I am in my chaffeur's uniform with gold Roller.

Another Lichfield picture of me – looking sophisticated!
Ron loves this photo.

Poor Lady Jane, she was so nice. She liked Reggie but she adored Ron. She had her hair deliberately cut like mine, and at one point, when she had to move out of her house, she wanted to come and live with me, or in a trailer in my garden. No, I said.

Unfortunately we haven't seen Lady Jane for a while, not since a New Year's Eve party given by a lovely man called Geoff Allen. He was a very wealthy man – he sold his mansion to Bill Wyman – and after he died they wrote in the papers that he was the brains behind the Great Train Robbery.

At the time Geoff had a massive house in Suffolk and Lady Jane was his house guest. He invited all sorts to this New Year's Eve party – there were posh people, normal people – like me, Charlie Kray, Flanagan and Harry – and then there were some real scumbags. I mean, mega-scumbags. Lady Jane didn't know anyone there, so she came up to us to say hello.

The clock struck midnight and we all kissed and said Happy New Year and Lady Jane, bless her, turned around to the man standing next to her, a real scumbag with a big scar on his face, and said in her posh voice: 'Ooh, Happy New Year!'

He swung around. 'What are you looking at, slag?! What did you say to me?!'

Poor Lady Jane! She was horrified! And me and Flanagan were looking away and trying not to laugh.

A little later she went up to the loo and by pure bad chance who was there waiting to go in when she came out but the very same scumbag!

'Get out of the way, slag!' he growled.

The next thing we see is poor Lady Jane juggling and struggling with five huge suitcases in the big front hall and hurrying out of the door! She'd packed her bags and she was off! And we haven't seen her since. A shame. She was very good fun, Lady Jane.

So much has happened since I became Mrs Kray, but one of the good things is that I have made some great friends. There's Flanagan, Geraldine Charles and Jackie, to name just three. I met Jackie through her husband Brynley Jones from Wales. He once came third in the Mr Universe contest and he'd been in prison with Reggie. He came to our wedding party at the Hilton. Jackie couldn't be there because she was heavily pregnant and, in fact, she gave birth to their daughter Carly the following day.

Brynley invited me down to Wales to meet Jackie and we became great friends – so much so that she named her second daughter Katie after me. Although Katie hasn't been christened I am her unofficial godmother and I'm not biased, of course, but she is the loveliest three-year-old you'll ever meet!

What Brynley and Jackie did by naming their daughter after me was very special, and I'll never forget that.

And I can't write about friends without mentioning Harry. He is my best friend and I'm very lucky to have him. Friends don't come much better than Harry and I admit that being my friend has landed him in hot water more than once.

For example, there was the matter of the shotgun. Harry borrowed a shotgun from a local scrap dealer when that madman Steve was coming to kill me. The problem was that after he had been caught Harry put the shotgun in the boot of his car and forgot all about it. Months later the police were on the doorstep to give us a spin – search the house. They suspected Harry of something or other which, needless to say, he wasn't involved in.

They found nothing until they looked in the boot of his car. And there was the shotgun. Since they were the same officers who'd seen me while that man was after me they knew full well why Harry had the shotgun.

But equally they couldn't very well ignore it, and they charged him with possession. Before long Harry was up before the beak. He didn't want to say that he had it in case the madman turned up to get me because that would have been possession with intent. So he was in something of a dilemma.

'Why were you in possession of this shotgun?' said the beak.

Harry thought quickly. 'Duck shooting,' he said. 'I was going duck shooting.'

Unfortunately the beak was very much the huntin', shootin' and fishin' type.

He paused. 'But, Mr Howard, it isn't the season for duck shooting.'

'I didn't realize that,' said Harry. 'I'm a novice.'

The prosecution wanted a custodial sentence, but he was just fined and put on probation. Even so, that's what I call a friend! Shortly afterwards it was Harry's birthday and he celebrated with some mates in the local pub. I arranged for a cake to be delivered to the party. It was in the shape of a shotgun and on it was iced: 'Happy Birthday Harry Boy...' and underneath: 'Duck Shooting My Arse!'

There are enemies, there are friends and fans and there is family. The best family news we had this year was the marriage of my younger sister Maggie to Ron's best friend in Broadmoor, Charlie Smith, who was the best man at our wedding.

Ron and I are really happy for them. It was a bit of a surprise. The last thing we expected when we introduced them was that they'd end up getting married.

Ron introduced me to Charlie when I first started visiting Broadmoor. Young Charlie, we call him, and he is only thirty-three, although he's been in there since he was about eighteen. Charlie was put on Ron's secure ward when he first arrived and they've been friends ever since.

He's a been a great companion over the years and Ron has really encouraged him in a career in music. Charlie plays the guitar and writes songs. He's made a few tapes of his music and Ron has always told him to believe that he has a future. And now, with Maggie, I think he does.

But there was no way that Ron and I went out of our way to get Maggie and Charlie together. It never occurred to us. Charlie's got a few friends and he has a few visitors but one day Ron said to me, 'Charlie hasn't got any visits lined up for the next week or so. Can't you bring one of your friends to visit him?'

I know how much visits mean to all of them, so I said OK. I couldn't think who but Maggie had come to stay with me so I asked her. She said yes, she wouldn't mind, and anyway she wanted to say hello to Ron because she hadn't seen him in a while.

So Maggie drove up with me. What we didn't realize was that as soon as they clapped eyes on each other that was that – they fell bang in love! Maggie gave up her home in Hampshire suburbia – her husband was a Navy man. Obviously they hadn't been very happy for some time. She left there, moved to Maidstone and in with me, and she and Charlie got married on 14 June.

The doctors say Charlie's coming on really well and hopefully it won't be long before he's out.

As for the rest of the family, Reggie is fine, although as the years go by it must be hard for him to keep his spirits up. But sometimes he amazes me. The last time I spoke to him on the phone he said he'd just got up and had a cold shower. 'The sun is shining, Kate. It's a beautiful day. It's great to be alive!' That stopped me from moaning!

# *THEN*

CHAPTER NINE

# *Taking Care of Business*

Business. Business first. Business always. That's how it's always been for Ronnie and Reggie, and that's how it always will be. And, in a way, I think that it's business that's kept them going all these years – that and the support of their friends, family and each other.

Ron is very secretive about his business, he always has been. So is Reg.

I was only a child when Ronnie and Reggie were running their businesses in London, but Ron has talked to me about what happened. He and Reggie remember the old days vividly. They don't regret what they did. It was business.

Even Nipper Read had to admit in his book: 'When the evidence about the butchery of the defenceless Jack McVitie came out in 1968 it seemed quite terrible. Now, nearly twenty-five years later, it seems we have heard tales which, if not worse, were at least as bad.'

Much has been written about the twins' love of violence – especially Ronnie's so-called love of violence – and, of course, about Ronnie's madness. But Ron says he didn't do what he did because he was mad. It was business. Yes, at times he suffered from mental illness and yes, at times that illness made him feel paranoid. But that isn't what made him shoot George Cornell. That isn't what made him sometimes resort to hurting people.

That was business.

In the world Reggie and Ronnie were living and working in it was survival of the fittest. Ronnie and Reggie were the fittest. In that sort of world you had to make people respect you. And people did respect Ron and Reg. They still do. Ronnie and Reggie regarded themselves as soldiers in a war.

Reggie described it well in his book, *Born Fighter*. He wrote:

> People still ask me today if I feel any remorse for the crime I committed. I have complex thoughts on this matter, not so much on the actual subject of remorse, but about why the establishment expects criminals to feel remorse for murder while at the same time expecting the soldier at war to feel victorious. Let's put it this way: if I had not killed Jack McVitie he might be writing this instead of me, and I might be where he is.
>
> In comparison, soldiers fighting in the Falklands, say, could justifiably pick out an Argentinian soldier on the skyline and squeeze the trigger. That would be the end of the Argentinian, who would most probably be a loving family man and not a villain like McVitie. The difference between the two individuals is like chalk and cheese, saint and sinner. And still, no one would ask the British soldier in the act of war if he felt any remorse for killing.
>
> If it was a matter of choice, I would sooner see the loss of the McVities of this world than the

> deaths of innocent young soldiers, plucked from the joys of life by the bullets of war.
>
> As human beings we've all got our failings and one day we will all be judged.

It was business.

Ron was asked by a researcher what his feelings were about the violence the twins showed to other villains in the 1950s and 1960. He said:

> I never felt sorry for anyone who got hurt. They deserved it, otherwise it wouldn't have happened. We didn't enjoy violence, we tried to avoid it, but we had to use it sometimes.
>
> One fella called me a fat slob so I had to do him. I went into the toilet and told someone I wanted to speak to him. As he came in, I cut him with a knife. He had to have plastic surgery.
>
> Another time, a straight man came to see me and he told me that a fella from Mile End had broken his daughter's nose because she wouldn't have sex with him. She was only fifteen. The Mile End fella also broke a seventeen-year-old boy's jaw in three places. So I phoned this fella up and told him I wanted to see him up Esmerelda's Barn. He was a dirty little rat. So I thought I'd set an example with him . . .
>
> We've both been violent in our time, me and Reggie, but we never liked it. It's like soldiers in the war, SAS and that. They're not violent people really but they have to use it. Our Uncle Albert

told me he shot a few people when he was in the Army, yet he was the most placid man I've ever met. He wouldn't have hurt a fly.'

Ron was, and is, respected because he was – and still is – fearless. Nothing and no one frightens him. When he met the Mafia bosses in New York, when he was confronted by villains at home who were out to get him, he showed no fear.

He never raises his voice, he never shouts threats, but still today people think twice about upsetting Ron. There's no bullshit about Ron. If he says he'll do something, he will. If he says he won't, he won't. If he does a deal he sticks to it. He's a man of honour.

And that's what he can't stand in other people – if they say one thing and do another. Both the twins are very loyal to their friends. People look after you, you look after them. He told me a story quite recently which I thought showed what a good friend he was – and how fearless he was.

Big Pat Connolly was a member of the Firm and a friend of Ron's. One day a man called Richie Anderson rang Ron. He was a much respected and feared gangster who ran businesses in the Gorbals area of Glasgow.

'Ron, Big Pat Connolly is a grass,' he said.

'What did you say?' said Ron.

'Big Pat Connolly is a grass.'

'Pat is a loyal and good friend,' said Ron. 'I'm coming up to Scotland to see you to tell you that to your face.'

Ron left London and went to Scotland and he travelled alone. He could easily have taken one or two of the Firm along as protection, but he chose not to. He got the plane to Glasgow and he was met at the airport by Richie Anderson and four of his men. Big men.

They got into cars and drove into Anderson's territory.

'Now,' said Ron, 'say to me again what you said on the phone.'

'He's a grass.'

'Big Pat Connolly is not a grass and I am here to tell you he is not. Stop the car here. You can do whatever it is you're planning to do to me. But I can tell you I'll do my best against all of you.'

The men looked at him and the driver kept driving. They pulled up outside a pub. They all went in and sat down and had a drink.

'Now,' said Ron. 'Do you want to tell me again?'

Richie Anderson paused. 'No,' he said. 'We don't want a row with you. You've come up here to tell us in person that's he's not a grass – that's good enough for us.' And then Richie gave Ron some cufflinks as a memento – two gold lions – which he still has today and Anderson's firm drove him back to the airport. In one piece.

I spoke to Richie Anderson on the phone recently. He now lives in London.

'We couldn't believe it when Ron came up to Glasgow alone,' said Richie. 'After that, there were many other times I saw Ron when his courage was very impressive. He wasn't frightened of anyone. Everyone had great respect for him.'

I'm not being funny when I say Ron is one of the most honest people I've ever met. If I read in the newspapers about something he's supposed to have done in the old days I ask him: 'Ron, did you really do that, you didn't did you?'

'Yes, I did,' he'll say. Or 'No, I didn't.' And I believe him. The twins have put their hands up to their crimes. The trouble is because of their reputation they got blamed for so many things they didn't do.

I asked Ron about Freddie Mills.

Freddie was the most famous boxer of his day, a light-weight world champion, a hero. After his retirement from the boxing game he became a showbusiness celebrity and opened his own nightclub, the Freddie Mills Nite Spot in Goslett Yard, Soho.

On Saturday, 24 July 1965 he spent most of the day quietly at his home in Denmark Hill, south London with his wife Chrissie and two daughters, Susan and Mandy, apparently pottering about quite happily and doing his garden.

In the evening he went to his club as usual. In the early hours of the Sunday morning his wife found him slumped in his car in Goslett Yard, dead from a rifle shot through the eye.

It was a strange case. The coroner's verdict was that he had taken his own life, but to the people who knew him best that didn't make any sense.

All kinds of stories started circulating, stories about Freddie's alleged homosexual affairs, his supposed money troubles. People said he'd been murdered. And, of course, since Ron and Reg were London's leading gangsters at the time, some people also pointed the finger at them.

And the finger has remained pointed in their direction for nearly thirty years.

But only two years ago leading boxing journalist Tony Van den Bergh wrote in his book *Who Killed Freddie Mills?*:

> One can only consider that the coroner's verdict was, from the police point of view, an extremely convenient one. They were already heavily involved with the most complex investigations into gang warfare in London and the possibility of a Mafia invasion. Further inquiries into this case might well have resulted in their having to expose more about their own operations than they would have wished. A verdict of suicide might well have been one they were ready to accept, in spite of the questions it left unanswered. And by the time Nipper Read reopened the case, years had passed and the trail was cold.
>
> If Mills, then, didn't pull the trigger, who did? [. . .] There is no sound evidence against either the Krays or the Richardsons. The Krays had become convenient scapegoats who could safely be blamed for any unsolved crimes . . .

Ron, of course, has always been well aware of the stories that have done the rounds, the story that he pulled the trigger, even the story that he was involved in a homosexual affair with Freddie Mills. But he has told me his story and I believe him.

'I never had a sexual relationship with him, Kate,' he said. 'Never. Of course I knew him. He was a nice fella and a great boxer. But I would never have a sexual relationship with a man.'

I understood what Ron meant by that. Ron has never made a secret of the fact that he's bisexual and has had sexual relationships with young men. But all his boyfriends have been young men. He wouldn't have a sexual relationship with a man. And Freddie Mills was a man.

Ron's bisexuality is his affair and in no way is Ron a camp, gay man. He hates all that camp prancing about. He can't stand it. He is a bisexual who has enjoyed relationships with younger men. But never a man like Freddie Mills.

'And I certainly didn't shoot him. That was just like so many other things, so many old wives' tales, put around by slags.'

Ron is convinced that some people put these stories about simply because they want Ron and Reg kept behind bars. They're afraid of Ron and Reg getting out because of all the ridiculous stories they've spread about them over the years.

What they don't understand is that Ron and Reg hear these stories and of course it affects them. Because they've been away for so long, people think of them as some kind of fantasy figures. People think they can say what they like. It doesn't count because the twins don't exist. They've disappeared for good.

But Ron and Reg are flesh and blood and they have feelings like anyone else. Far too many people don't think before they speak. Ron and Reg are not on the moon – they're in Berkshire and Hampshire. They hear the radio, read the papers and watch the television.

And how would these people feel if they were the Krays and they heard some of the things that are written or spoken about them? Only the other day I was furious when Ron told me that he'd been listening to the radio and up popped a so-called friend who confidently told the interviewer: 'They'll never let Ronnie out.' If you'd been banged up for twenty-five years, how would you feel when you heard that?

Some of the stories about the twins are amazing.

Ron refuses to comment on the whereabouts of Frank Mitchell, the 'Mad Axeman' they sprung from Dartmoor. Ron and Reg were tried for his murder. Both denied it and they were both acquitted. Ask Ron where he is now and he shrugs and says: 'How am I supposed to know?' Then he jokes, 'He's probably alive and well and living in Bosnia!'

But only the other day I was asked by a man I met at a party: 'Is it true he was fed to the snorters at a pig farm in the country?'

As for Jack 'The Hat' McVitie's body, one story was that it had been weighted down and thrown overboard a boat in the bay of Whitstable in Kent. I asked Ron about that because I have a friend who lives there and she didn't like the idea of walking her dogs on the mudflats at low tide in case they accidentally dug him up!

Ron was able to reassure her that she could walk the dogs without worrying. So, where? I don't know.

Ron said to me the other day that he still has no regrets. At least, he regrets being banged up for twenty-five years, of course, but that's the one thing he regrets. But he is grateful for the excellent medical treatment he's received. That has made life bearable.

I was fascinated by the film *The Krays*. As you can imagine, watching it was a weird experience for me – and Ron, too, I think. Most of Ron's friends I've talked to who were around the twins in the 1960s thought it wasn't a bad portrayal of their life then – although they all grouse about some inaccuracy or other and they all thought the film-makers made life seem more sensational than it was at the time.

But as Ron's friend, Alec Steen, the boxing promoter, said: 'What can you expect? It was only a movie, after all.'

I was invited to the première and went along to the party, which I didn't enjoy as much as I could have done because it all happened during that time when I wasn't feeling well. At the party, and before the film in the foyer, I couldn't help feeling paranoid with all those people going: 'Whisper, whisper... look, that's her... that's Ronnie's wife...'

As soon as I could, I took a video of the film up to Broadmoor for Ron.

'What did you think of it?' I asked him.

'Not much,' he said. 'I put it on, then I realized it was nearly half-past five. So I took it out and watched "Neighbours" instead!'

Later, he sat through the entire film. Neither Ron nor Reg liked the way Billie Whitelaw played their mother, Violet.

'She never used to swear like that,' said Ron.

But he told me he got a real shock when 'Cornell', actor Steven Berkoff, came on screen.

'I couldn't believe it. Berkoff was brilliant,' said Ron. 'It was like seeing Cornell all over again. He captured him perfectly, the way he walked, talked, his mannerisms. It was uncanny.'

'So did you want to shoot him again?'

Ron gave me one of his looks. He had no comment to that!

A lot of rubbish has been written about the 'millions' Ron and Reg picked up from the people who made the film, *The Krays*. Millions! You must be joking! They should be so lucky! *I* should be so lucky! I'm not at liberty to say how much they got, but it wasn't millions – it wasn't one million – it wasn't anything like it.

Of course the twins made some money out of the film, and quite right too! Everyone else has made money out of them. 'Blood money', Ron calls it.

But whatever Ron got, most of it he gave away. He gave away forty-two grand in two weeks – to charities, to friends, to people he thought needed it. Forty-two grand? Yes, forty-two grand.

I've got an old building-society book here from back in 1988 when I was handling Ron's money for him. We're with the Woolwich. The entries are typical – I wrote down what everything was for, so I could remember it all.

'Hundred pounds sick kid'... 'fifty pounds —'s daughter'... 'hundred pounds for — in — prison'... 'two hundred...'

As soon as it came in, out it went again. No wonder I practically went right around the bend organizing it all.

Sometimes the account went down to as little as ten pounds and then up to, well, a bit more than that. Most of the time I'm skint, but here's another entry: 'Kate two hundred'. Sometimes Ron will give me something to tide me over – when he's got it. But I don't expect money from him. He's not in regular employment, is he?!

Ron and Reg still need money to live, even if they are in prison. They get some social security, and money for any work they do inside, but that doesn't amount to much and they need more than that.

Ron has a bank account at Broadmoor so he can buy things from the shop there: toiletries, books, cigarettes. Reggie's given up smoking and I admire him for that. But Ron loves his fags. Whatever doctors say – and of course they nag him about it just as they nag everyone else – I can't see him ever giving up.

Then there's the tea, coffee and biscuits he buys when people visit him and the alcohol-free lager he likes.

Ron also buys all his own clothes. He's a very smart man and always impeccably turned out. Handmade shoes, made-to-measure suits, the finest shirts, gold cufflinks. And a gold watch – if he hasn't given it away.

They used to call Ron 'The Watchman' because he gave away so many watches. I saved up three and a half grand to buy a watch as a wedding present for Ron. It was beautiful – eighteen-carat gold Omega with thirty-two brilliant white diamonds around the outside. On the back I had inscribed: 'All my love, Kate. 6.11.89', the date of our wedding.

Ron loved that watch. He said it was the best watch he'd ever seen and everyone admired it. That was the trouble – someone would admire it, so Ron would give it to them! I went mad, I really told him off.

'But that was a wedding present, Ron.'

'I couldn't help it,' he said. 'I don't know why I did it. I just thought "I've got so much and he hasn't got anything" so he could have it.'

Sometimes he leaves me speechless. I mean Ron hasn't got anything, he hasn't even got his liberty, for heaven's sake! One time he actually sold the watch because he was skint. Someone said to him: 'It's a lovely watch, Ron. I think I could get ten thousand for it, especially with the engraving on the back.' And Ron went: 'Ten thousand!' So he handed over the watch and told the man to sell it. But the man felt bad about it, so he rang me. 'I could tell Ron didn't really want to sell it,' he said. 'He felt bad about it. So do I.'

I went to meet the man and he gave me the watch back. The next time I went up to see Ron I had it safely in my handbag.

'Come on, me old Dutch,' he said. 'Sit down, I've got something to tell you...'

'Oh, yeah?'

'Look, I was skint, I needed some money so I've sold the watch...'

'No you haven't,' I said. And produced it out of my handbag.

'That's a liberty!' said Ron. 'Him ringing you up. I told him not to.' But I think he was glad to have it back.

That was the fifth time I retrieved that watch. Perhaps Ron just wasn't meant to have it. When I needed money for a deposit on my flat Ron didn't have any, so he gave me the watch instead.

I gave it to someone to sell and he gave me two thousand pounds for my deposit and said he'd give me the balance when it had actually been sold. But then some girl who worked for him was carrying it in London and she got mugged. So I never did get the balance – and someone, somewhere, is running around wearing Ronnie Kray's watch and they probably don't even know it!

Now the only wedding present Ron has left from me is a tie pin. I bought a huge diamond and had it set in a heart of sapphires and on the back I had engraved 'Love Kate'. Four years later Ron has still got it . . . I hope.

These days there is no Firm. In fact, Ron told me that if he'd had his way he would have sacked most of the Firm well before he and Reggie were nicked.

'If I had my time over again I wouldn't have had most of them around me. Most of them turned out to be grasses,' said Ron.

But Ron and Reg have some very good friends who see them regularly, friends who I know would protect me if necessary.

The twins are still very well informed about what goes on, they've got their fingers on the pulse of what's happening.

But these days their business is more likely to involve a book or film about the Krays than anything else. People do go to them with some extraordinary business ideas.

'We're going into the mirror business, Kate,' Ron said the other day.

'The what?'

'We're going to have ours faces engraved on mirrors...'

'Like Elvis Presley?' I asked.

Ron laughed. 'Yeah, just like Elvis Presley!'

It keeps them interested and amused. And it earns them a few bob.

But I don't believe that money – money for the sake of having it, money to show off with, or money to hoard away – has ever been what has truly motivated Ronnie and Reggie. They lived well, they wore nice clothes, drove nice cars, lived in nice flats, looked after their family and friends and travelled a bit.

But no one could say they lived in a grand, flashy way when they did have money on the outside. And if Ron was given a million pounds tomorrow he wouldn't salt it away in some bank. The first thing he'd do is make me sit down and make a list of all the people he wanted to send some to!

I think what interested Ronnie and Reggie was the making of money. The business of it. It's the same even today... if you want to put a smile on Ronnie's face you bring him a bit of business.

# *NOW*

## CHAPTER TEN

# *Down at the Funny Farm*

The phone rang in March of this year. It was Broadmoor.

'Kate, we don't want you to get upset but Ron's collapsed in his room. We've taken him to the infirmary – we're not sure. It could be a heart attack. But don't panic.'

Panic? I went into total panic. 'I've got to talk to Reggie, I must get through to Reggie.' That was the first thing. That was the most important thing.

I rang the nick, told them who I was, and asked them to tell him it was an emergency and could he ring me urgently.

He was on the phone within a few minutes.

I was crying but I said: 'Don't get upset, Reg . . .'

'What's the matter? What's the matter? It's Ron, isn't it? I know it's Ron.'

'He collapsed this morning. They think he's had a heart attack.'

Reggie was now crying too. I told him I'd ring him as soon as I heard anything.

Broadmoor rang again and said they were doing tests on Ron . . . They told me I couldn't see Ron; he wasn't well enough, but to ring back in an hour.

It was one of the longest hours of my life.

'It's not his heart,' they said when I called back. 'We think it could be a brain tumour, so we're doing a brain scan on him.'

It was all going from bad to worse. I rang Reggie and told him. We were both in a terrible state. Then finally they let Ron phone me from the infirmary.

'Are you all right?'

'They're doing tests on me. Don't worry. I'm all right, but I don't feel very well . . . Got any news?'

Typical! I was worried sick, but the final result turned out to be good instead of bad. The doctors discovered that they'd been giving him too much medication and that had caused him to collapse. Sometimes, with age, the kind of schizophrenia that Ron suffers from can burn itself out. And that's what had happened to Ron. It didn't mean he was cured, but it did mean that he was apparently on the road to recovery.

Once he got over his collapse, the doctors stopped all his medication completely. They had to get the new balance right so they had to start from scratch. I didn't know what to expect and Ron didn't either – he's been taking these drugs for so long. But when I went up to see him he looked great and he felt it too.

'How are you?'

'I feel absolutely marvellous, marvellous,' he said.

He was sound as a pound, sharp as a tack. It's not that when I saw him before he sat there with his eyes glazed or anything like that, but I definitely noticed a difference.

But after a while he began to feel a little bit paranoid and he doesn't like those feelings, so the doctors gave him something.

Before I married Ron I had to talk to his doctors. They wanted me to understand as much as I could about his illness – and to know what I was letting myself in for.

Ron is a chronic paranoid schizophrenic. Even the experts are not sure what causes it – or what fully cures it, if anything. They think it's most likely due to a chemical imbalance in the brain, that it can be triggered by a stressful event in someone's life like the death of a parent or close relative, and that it usually strikes in adolescence when the hormones in the body are already going through enormous upheaval.

Ron told me he was about twenty-two when he first began to feel unwell, and he thinks the trigger was the death of one of the women he loved most in the world, his Aunt Rose.

Schizophrenics suffer from hallucinations and/or delusions. In Ron's case he doesn't hallucinate, but he suffers from delusions of persecution. He gets paranoid and has feelings, for no particular reason, that people are intent on hurting or even killing him.

It is hell to suffer from mental illness. My nervous breakdown was bad enough, but Ron has suffered for most of his life and I really feel for him. He's had electric-shock treatment and years of drugs. I don't know how he's lived through it all. I don't envy him.

Most schizophrenics are not violent people – like Ron, they're usually very mild-mannered, quietly-spoken and sometimes withdrawn. The illness can strike anyone from any walk of life. The illness doesn't differentiate between rich or poor, black or white, Muslim or Christian. But it doesn't have to last a lifetime. More than a third of people who've suffered a schizophrenic attack never relapse into another one, and many middle-aged schizophrenics become what they call, in the jargon of mental illness, quiescent, burnt-out cases.

So when Ron told me that they said he was 'burnt out' I knew what he meant and it's a good sign. He was made up about it. Me too.

But, unfortunately, in the months that followed there have been setbacks.

The worst, of course, was what happened between Ron and Kiernender. Now the most important thing is to get Ron better. It's a slow job and the doctors have told me that they have got to sort out Ron's medication. Ron isn't the same old Ron yet and it's a long road, but we'll get there in the end.

What happened was a shock. But Ron wasn't right in the weeks before, especially after Charlie's rubbish was printed. He was quiet, suspicious, wary.

I have always known when Ron's been 'going into one'. I can tell the minute I see him. When he goes into one it's not dramatic like someone having an epileptic fit or anything like that. He's just different. I look into his eyes and they're empty. It's a certain look on his face. On the visit he'll be very quiet, he doesn't say a lot, he doesn't trust anyone.

He tells me later how he felt. Sometimes when he's been in one he's been a bit mean to me, but afterwards, when he's come out of it, he'll say: 'I was just feeling funny, Kate. I didn't mean it.'

When he's gone into one there's very little I can do, and that hurts. I can tell how lonely he is. Mental illness is lonely. It's not as if I pinch you and it hurts but you can cope with it because you know that when I stop pinching, it will stop hurting. When you're hurting in your mind you can't get away from it; it's there all the time. It must be a dreadful feeling.

Ron doesn't want to be like that, of course he doesn't. Would you? If someone was going to kick you in the shins, you know it's going to hurt, so you don't want it to happen. It's the same with Ron. When he feels he's going into one he knows how it feels, and he doesn't want to feel like that so he'll always take his drugs.

If you've got a headache you take a pill for it. Ron's exactly the same. So when he goes into one he'll take whatever drugs the doctors give him. Then he likes to be alone. He doesn't want people going on at him, pulling or pushing at him. He doesn't want people going up to see him and talking a lot of old crap. He needs space. After medical help, he's left alone, he's old and wise enough to handle it for himself.

He used to have to take a drug called Largactil, but then they put him on Stemetil to calm his nerves. On top of that he had to take Disipal to counteract the side effects of the Stemetil – often people suffer from a loss of muscle control which means they make involuntary movements. Then they also gave him a Modecate injection once a fortnight, which stopped him getting bad dreams and depression.

After taking all those drugs for so long you can imagine how apprehensive we were about them cutting it all down. But it seemed to be the best thing that could have happened to him.

Now Ron is on a variety of drugs, as the doctors deem necessary. Anybody who says that if they let Ron out he wouldn't take whatever drugs the doctors prescribed are talking total rot. Of course he would. He doesn't want to feel ill and he knows that as long as he takes the medicines they tell him to take he's OK.

Ron gets on well with his doctors and they all seem to like him. I see them occasionally, and other members of the staff too, but only if there's something particular they want to talk to me about or if Ron's not been too well.

Some wives go to the patients' tribunals and I could, too, but I don't. The tribunals are meetings where they assess the patients' progress and debate whether or when they're ever going to let them out. Patients can have one every year if they choose, and every three years it's compulsory.

Ron tells me not to come because he says it's a waste of time. However well he's doing he feels they won't let him out because he's a Kray. And they certainly won't let him out until Reggie's out. I'd be happy to go, but he says no.

In fact, the staff did call me once. There was nothing really wrong, they said, but they wanted to get Ron motivated. Well, a nice bit of business always does that but I don't think that's what they had in mind!

They said that Ron spent most of his days staying on the ward, walking up and down the corridors or maybe going to the day room where you can read or play cards and socialise.

'We've got to do something,' they said. 'Brush the cobwebs away!'

Cobwebs, indeed! I don't see many cobwebs on Ron. 'Don't make him make a basket,' I said, 'because I can tell you here and now he won't do it!'

They laughed. 'No,' they said, 'nothing like that. We just want him to get interested in doing something. Talk to him and see if there's anything he'd like to do.'

So I did.

Ron was mad. 'Don't think they're going to make me work, because I'm not going to! I haven't done a day's manual work in my life and I'm not going to start now!'

'If you had the choice of doing something, what would you do?' I said.

'I wouldn't mind going down to the garden,' he said.

'Well, try it.'

'I'm not going to work in the garden, I won't do it!' he said. He is a stubborn old sod.

'Just go for one day. Wouldn't you like to be outside? You'll get a suntan, get nice and brown. Just try it for one day.'

Reluctantly he agreed. 'One day. Just one,' he said.

But he liked it. 'Marvellous,' he said after the first time.

'What did you do?'

'Well, I did a bit of watering ... and then I went to the shed for a chat.' Some people have since written that Ron has become a really passionate gardener, merrily digging away with his garden spade. That makes me laugh. What crap! Ron's idea of gardening most of the time is to sit in the sun having a fag. But at least it gets him outside, although he'll only do it when the weather's nice!

Last summer he got really tanned. In the summer they sometimes allow visits out on the verandah. I was sitting there waiting for him and he came out wearing a lovely silver-grey suit, a crisp white and blue doubled-cuffed shirt, his gold cufflinks, watch and crocodile shoes.

I just looked at him. When people have been inside for a long time they get a greyness in their skin, but he'd lost that. He looked really great.

'You look like you've just stepped off a bleeding yacht!' I said. Ron laughed.

But Ron's future in horticulture may now be doubt.

'Three pounds a week!' he said to me the other day. 'For three years I've been working for them and that's what they're paying me! What do they think I am – a paperboy? I didn't work on the outside so I'm not working on the inside. I'm nearly sixty – I'm going to retire . . .' He does make me laugh . . . 'Don't laugh, Kate, this is serious. Three pounds a week! . . .'

Everyone calls Broadmoor the 'Funny Farm'. It is, I suppose, a funny place, full of funny people, but most of all it is a quiet place, very calm and peaceful. Most of the time Ron is reasonably content. He has his own room now and there's reinforced glass at the windows instead of bars, so at least he can look out over the countryside.

The new Governor, Mr Franey, has made a lot of changes for the better. He wants to change the place from being a Victorian asylum to a modern, secure hospital. He wants to treat the patients as human beings.

He works on the idea that if you behave, you'll be all right. You can have privileges, but you have to work for them and prove you won't abuse them. All fair enough, Ron says.

For years Ron never gave them any trouble, so he earned the right to decorate his bedroom as he chose, in yellow and peach with some floral curtains and a matching bedspread.

He's got a cassette player and a television. As a high-profile prisoner he was one of the last to get his own TV and he had to prove that he could keep the noise down so it wouldn't disturb anyone else.

Ron reads a bit, mainly biographies, and he enjoys listening to classical music – the opera *Madame Butterfly* is his favourite. He watches the news on television every day and he's a fan of 'Neighbours' and old English films, especially war films.

His usual day starts at just before seven, when the doors are unlocked, and it finishes at nine when they're banged up for the night. The time in between is spent cleaning his room, then maybe doing the garden three or four times a week, and medical treatment. He walks the corridors to keep fit and he visits the day room for a smoke and to chat to the other patients. He has regular visits from me and his friends.

And, of course, he has his letters to write. He gets about a hundred a day, and he can't possibly answer them all. But he tries to reply to as many as possible. It costs a bloody fortune in postage.

Every hour of the day is accounted for. It's all quite regimented. I suppose it has to be.

> 6.55 to 7.20: Patients wash and dress and make their beds.
> 7.20 to 8: Breakfast.
> 8 to 8.30: Go to day room or occupation room.

Day in day out, year in year out, the routine rarely changes. That would be enough to drive me mad.

Sometimes they have social evenings when the patients – the men and the women – can get together. There's soft drinks and music, even a disco. In all the years he's been there, Ron has only gone along a few times. He's really not the type of man to enjoy a good rave!

Ron likes his privacy; he keeps himself to himself most of the time. But, of course, he's got to know some of the other patients.

Often in the garden Ron used to see Jennifer and June Gibbons. They were known as the 'Silent Twins', because for many years they didn't talk to anyone except each other and when they did talk to each other no one could understand a word they said. It was as if they had a secret language and they could communicate telepathically.

Ron really liked them, and he used to get me to send them flowers on their birthday. He was terribly upset in March when one of the twins, Jennifer, died. The twins were just being allowed out to a halfway house when she collapsed. How her sister, June, copes now I don't know. Ron sent flowers to the funeral.

In the next room to Ron is the man the papers dubbed the 'Yorkshire Ripper', Peter Sutcliffe. Ron doesn't have much to do with him. I see him sometimes in the hall when I'm visiting Ron and Sutcliffe's wife Sonia is up to see him.

He looks just like the picture they always use of him in the papers, except now he's got a big scar down one side of his face. When he was in Parkhurst someone apparently went for him and rammed a broken glass coffee jar in his face.

When you meet him it's his eyes you notice. His eyes

are hollow, empty. It's as if he's looking at you but his eyes aren't there.

The latest I've heard is that Sonia is filing for divorce. We were never friends, but I used to say hello to her when I saw her in the Ladies' or the hall. I felt sorry for her. The first time I saw her was in the waiting room. She was sitting there, a mouselike little person, all on her own, with sunglasses on, her head held down as if she was too scared to look at anybody.

I'm always surprised when I find out what some of the Broadmoor patients have done. They're so sweet, some of them, they come up and give you a kiss or leave you a little present on the table in the hall.

There was one lovely young bloke who used to bring us coffee during visits. I said to Ron: 'Isn't he sweet?'

I later learned he was the 'Tottenham Rapist'. Oh.

Another time Ron was telling me that he'd met a man who gave him a really good shoulder massage.

'He has wonderful hands,' he says. 'He massages your shoulders and it really gets rid of all the tension.'

'What's he in for?' I asked casually.

'Oh, he strangled all his family. But he gives a great massage . . .'

The 'Stockwell Strangler' is on Ron's ward, too. Most of the time he just sits there staring at the lights.

Ron keeps himself to himself, but he likes to watch people. Once he was watching this man and he saw someone try to nick his sweets. Suddenly the man's face changed. He suddenly just turned, and you could see the madness in him. He's only a young man and he knows he's never going to come out. A lot of them are so sad, just sitting there. They're not even aware of life going on around them.

Some of the people Ron meets he likes. Some he despises. One man, Ron Saxon, Ron despised.

There are three nice black boys in the hospital called Mohammed Kamhmer, Cleveland Jones and Paul Wilson. They used to fetch and carry for Saxon, especially after he had a heart attack. They really liked him and Ron obviously thought that Saxon appreciated what they did for him.

But one day, when Ron commented to Saxon about how good they'd been to him, Saxon merely scoffed.

'They're black bastards,' he said. 'They're OK – but only good enough to be used.'

Ron was horrified. Racial prejudice is one of the things he hates most in the world. He told me that if Saxon had been a younger man he would have hurt him. After that Ron – my Ron – would have nothing to do with him.

Saxon had a second heart attack and died, and Ron refused to go to the funeral at Broadmoor. The only people who went were the three black boys.

'It just goes to show,' said Ron. 'It just proves to me how ignorant people can be, however old they are. They get old and they're still ignorant. I hate fascists.

'If Ron Saxon can see from beyond the grave – and I think he can – he would have seen these three coloured boys coming back to the ward after paying their respects to him at his funeral. And he would have seen tears in their eyes.'

Ron was upset about that. But sometimes he makes me laugh about his friends in Broadmoor. There are so many funny stories.

One of his friends is Bob Burnie, who was sent to Broadmoor after the screws split his head open during a ruck at the Scrubs. Ron likes him a lot.

Some of the others, of course, are completely nutty. There was the man they used to call the 'Bedspring Swallower', for obvious reasons. And another is a man called Mr Brown. He lives under the delusion that he's a doctor which, I suppose, isn't as bad as thinking he's Napoleon or Hitler.

When you want to make a phonecall from the ward you have to chalk your name on a board so it can be monitored. One day this bloke wrote on the board 'Doctor Brown'.

So Ron's friend, Bob, who was next in line, wrote 'Bob Burnie, OBE'. The 'doctor' was furious, and stormed off in high dudgeon. Ron and Bob, of course, were creased up with laughter. They get used to funny things happening all the time in Broadmoor. Once Ron was supposed to meet one of the coloured boys, Mohammed, in the day room. He found him fast asleep in the chair so he shook him to wake him up. Mohammed went berserk. He was terrified, and jumped on the chair.

'What's the matter with you?' says Ron.

'Oh Ron,' he said. 'It's you. Thank God. I was just having this really sexy dream that I was making love to this girl and her husband came in and found us. I thought for a moment you were the husband!'

On 8 May 1992 it was twenty-five years since Ron and Reg were locked up. I don't know how they've stood it all that time. In a way, it's been worse for Reg than for Ron. Ron was very pleased the day they took him to

Broadmoor – on 25 July 1979 – it was a good day, he says.

At least in Broadmoor Ron has had the medical treatment he needs – I'm sure that if they'd kept him in prison he wouldn't be as well as he is now. At least he gets lots of visits, he can wear his own clothes, he gets nice food and he can have some of his own possessions around him.

The latest thing he asked me to get him was a china cup and saucer for his tea. He was fed up with drinking out of mugs. But bone china, he said. It had to be fine bone china. Of course! Basically, if he has to be inside, at least he's in a hospital environment.

Reggie's had a very tough time. He can have more visits now and he's allowed to use the phone, but for a long, long time it was just two visits a month and no phone. Reg keeps himself very fit and he needs to. For years he's been moved around from prison to prison and because he's high-profile they move him in the middle of the night with no warning.

And whenever he gets to a new prison he has to prove himself all over again. There's always someone who wants to take him on because he's a Kray, take a pot shot at him, someone with no respect who thinks that by taking on a Kray he can prove he's big and tough.

He's not as young as he was, but he could still break someone's jaw if he had to.

Reg has had to endure so many disappointments, and most through no fault of his own. When he was in Lewes prison there was talk that they might move him to Ford prison in Hampshire. That's an open prison and would have made life much better for Reg. Also, it's one step nearer to getting out.

But Reg had a row with someone in Lewes and when that man came out he wanted to make trouble for Reg. So he rang up the Governor of the prison and told him: 'Reggie Kray's got a gun smuggled in and he's going to escape.'

Reg has been in prison for twenty-five bloody years. He's hardly going to smuggle a gun in at this stage of the game. After twenty-five years? What for?! He's nearly finished his sentence – he wouldn't do that. But even so there was a big security alert and they searched through all Reggie's things in his cell. Needless to say they found nothing.

Even the Governor said to Reggie: 'We know it's all a load of old cobblers but we've got to be seen to do it.' So in the middle of the night when Reggie was asleep they burst in and took him off to another cell. Then they shanghaied him out of there and for a while he was back in the Scrubs. Then they moved him on again, to Blundestone.

Another setback. And through no fault of Reggie's.

But we keep hoping, hoping that they'll let Reggie out soon. The twins have never moaned about their sentence, they've never whinged. Even now Ron says to me: 'There's a lot of people worse off than me. I'm not blind, I'm not crippled.' And Reggie is just the same. But they've done their time. They've paid for their crime. It makes me furious that they won't even consider letting them out. Reggie wouldn't cause any trouble if they let him out. If they let him out now he'd be out under licence, which means that if he was caught doing anything naughty he'd be sent back to prison for the rest of his life. He knows that. And do you really think that after twenty-five years inside that is something he would risk?

It's so bloody unfair. It's only because of the name Kray that they won't let them out. It's because they're famous. If Reggie Kray was called Joe Bloggs he would have been out years ago.

This isn't justice. I read in the paper the other day about a man who had tortured and killed his little baby. He was given two and a half years! Two and a half years! And no doubt he'll be out before that. Is that justice?

OK. Ron and Reg each killed a man. OK. They had to pay a price. But if you are going to say that for killing a man the price is thirty years in prison then it should be thirty years for every man who kills – not just for the ones with a famous name like Kray.

When you think of some of the sentences that have been passed on criminals over recent years, and then you compare what they did to the crimes of Ron and Reg, then I cannot for the life of me see the justice in it.

Even Nipper Read, in his book, said that what the Krays did was nothing compared to the terrible crimes which are committed today. And people who have done far worse things, like torturing and murdering children, are allowed out for the day – even Myra Hindley's alleged to have been out shopping.

But Reggie's never been allowed such a privilege. The only times he's been allowed out were for his mother's funeral and when they they've been moving him from prison to prison or to visit Ron.

And, as for my Ron, he can't even stroll in the garden on his own. What do they think he's going to do? Do a bunk? What, after all this time? Ron's not stupid.

In fact, Ron has been out a couple of times – to local hospitals for medical treatment. He's had a couple of operations on his ears and two months ago he had a hernia operation at Ascot hospital. But, even so, he didn't see much of the outside world.

'We drive through the countryside to the hospital and that's it,' says Ron. 'I'm sure if I'd been in London I would have noticed changes, but a tree is a tree is a tree in the 1960s or the 1990s.'

'I just get glimpses of things. Then I'm in hospital – and they give me an anaesthetic! Next thing I know I'm back in Broadmoor's infirmary.'

He was allowed out too for Violet's funeral. Ron hated it. It was like a circus, with all those people and photographers, and they deliberately chose the tallest prison officers they could find to escort Ron and Reg to make them look small in comparison.

Now Ron's nightmare is that he'll die inside. Shortly after our wedding, I visited a spiritualist. She didn't know who I was but the first thing she said was: 'Congratulations. You've just got married, haven't you? To an older man.'

I couldn't believe it. Then it got even spookier.

'There seems to be a lot of madness around this man. You used to see this man's elder brother before you met your husband.' True, because of course Reg is ten minutes older than Ron.

Then she told me that I would have a nervous breakdown and an operation on my stomach – both, as you know, true – but most important of all she said: 'I don't know if this makes sense to you, but I've got a lady coming through. Her name is the name of a flower. She's a no-nonsense type of woman. She has her sleeves rolled up and she can have a tear-up with a man, if necessary. She wants you to tell your husband that he won't die in there. She's adamant you must tell him he won't die in there.' The spiritualist was puzzled. 'Does that make sense to you?'

Oh yes, it made sense to me, and I wondered if it was Ron's mother Violet or his Aunt Rose who was coming through.

I just hope to God she's right and Ron does come out. We both know it would be a very slow process. Gradually they would move him within Broadmoor so he had more freedom, then perhaps they might allow him out just for an afternoon. I'd love to be able to take him out to a nice restaurant for lunch. Maybe we'd be allowed to have some time in that cottage in the grounds – and get to enjoy our conjugal rights!

'How do you feel about that, then?' I say to Ron.

'After twenty-five years? Take it or leave it,' he says. The old sod.

'They'll hear you screaming for mercy all over Broadmoor!' I say. 'You'll be screaming, "No more, no more! Get off! Get off!"'

In his darkest moments, Ron says: 'I'm never going to get out but I don't care.' And we've talked about death. I have strict instructions about his funeral – typically, he knows exactly what he wants. He doesn't want any old hearse; he wants a carriage drawn by two black horses wearing big black plumes to pull him through the East

End and then for him to be buried in the plot next to his mother in Chingford.

And he wants me to send a big wreath of white chrysanthemums which spell out his name: 'The Colonel'.

I say: 'Yes, you'd like to have me there all weeping and wailing in black – with all your little mistresses and boyfriends!'

I tell him that on the headstone I'm going to put: 'Here lies Ronnie Kray – a Ruthless Bastard' and Ron just laughs. I thought, I might just put on it: 'Got any news?'

But with any luck that's a long way off. I just hope that they let them out soon. Reggie first and then, please, Ron.

I'm not sure what Reg will do. There's so much he has to catch up on – but I know he'll be up at Broadmoor with his brother most of the time. Maybe Reggie will marry again when he comes out. He's had some blinding girlfriends since he's been inside. But he has never married. It would be good if he could find someone nice.

As for me, I can see me staying with Ron, whether he's in or out. So much has happened since I became Mrs Kray – good and bad – but I've never regretted marrying him, never. People say I've changed – even Harry says I've changed. I'm not as soft and trusting as I was. I'm busier and I'm less inclined to spend time on things that don't count. I hope people don't think I'm hard-nosed. I'm not. Just sometimes you have to be.

Why did I marry Ron? Because he came along at the right time, because he's security, because he's one of a kind, because there's no one else in the world like Ron, because he makes me laugh, because he drives me mad, but most of all because I love him. Maybe it's a funny kind of love. But it's love.

Arthur Daley calls his 'Her Indoors'. I call mine 'Him Inside'. Maybe that will change.

In his brighter moments Ron talks about coming out. Then, he says, 'We'll go on a tour around the world.' That sounds about right.

Then we'll buy a big house in the country. Ron loves the country and so do I.

We might keep a dog – Ron loves animals. I love them, too, but they don't often seem to take to me. Harry and I used to have a cockatiel and it would eat out of Harry's hand. When I tried that, the bloody thing just pecked me so we gave it to Harry's mum. Then we had two lovebirds in a cage.

'Don't forget you need some seed and water,' said the man in the pet shop.

'What did he say? They're called Sid and Walter?!' Well, that's what they were called after that! Ron loves that story.

So birds – and budgies – are out. Maybe a dog.

Our house will have a big tall wall around it. Ron needs his privacy, and even outside I know he'll need to feel he can keep his distance from people if he chooses. He won't like people to have easy access to him.

The house will have a lovely garden, although I doubt very much that I'll manage to get Ron gardening. But he'll enjoy sitting out there in the sun. He'll have what he wants: peace and quiet. And we'll be together.

And we've already decided what we're going to call our house. On a wooden plaque outside on the wall by the gate we'll put the name: Broadmoor.

CHAPTER ELEVEN

# *Postscript*

Since I wrote this book – and because of this book – my life has changed dramatically.

Throughout the summer of '93 I saw Ron two or three times a week and phoned him every evening at eight on the dot as usual. But by the Spring of 1994 there were no happy visits sitting outside on the visitors' terrace enjoying the sunshine. After the episode with Kiernender, Ron was confined to the intensive care of Abingdon Ward while the doctors tried to get the balance of his drugs right.

I worried about him. He was still feeling very poorly and, at times, paranoid. Sometimes we would laugh and joke and I'd see flashes of the old Ron, the Ron I knew and loved, but, on the whole, he was far more serious and occasionally he'd snap at me for no apparent reason. His doctors were ringing me twice a week about his progress and they told me not to get upset if Ron was sometimes distant and unfriendly. It was, they said, all part of his illness.

The hardback edition of this book was published in September 1993, and immediately I sent advance copies to Ronnie and Reggie. Reggie didn't comment at all – and he still hasn't. He didn't praise it – or slag it off. Nothing. Not a word.

Ron phoned me and I was waiting for him to say how much he loved it!

'You've let me down,' he said. I was flabbergasted! He had to be joking. What?!

'I don't like it.'

'Why?'

'It's too personal. Come up and see me.'

So, as soon as I could, I made the trip to Broadmoor and we talked. Ron wasn't upset in the slightest that I'd written about my love affair with Pa – he knew all along I was going to include that and it didn't bother him.

'What I don't like is you've shown a side of me that's too personal.'

I was stumped. I never imagined for one minute that my revelations would upset him. To the contrary, I thought he'd be pleased. I tried to explain:

'So many people write about you and write what they *think* you're like and what they *think* Reggie's like and most of the time they hardly know you. Sometimes they haven't even met you! I wanted to show what you're *really* like.'

And that was the truth. Ron was a gangster, he may be in Broadmoor, but he isn't the mad creature he's sometimes made out to be. He's intelligent and wise, quite sensitive and humorous at times, and I wanted to show that side of him.

'Rubbish,' said Ron. 'Don't kid a kidder!'

Stalemate. I was telling the truth but he didn't believe me.

So we had a bit of a barney for a short while.

'I might divorce you because of this,' said Ron.

'All right,' I said, confident he didn't mean it.

'I'll read it again,' he said and then, having got it all off his chest, he changed the subject and we were back to normal. We parted friends as usual. I was upset that what I'd written had upset Ron – that was the last thing in the world I'd intended – but in a way I could understand. All I'd wanted to do was tell the truth but I'd found it difficult to write – and then to read. It must have been hard for Ron to read about himself too.

Soon I was travelling all over the place giving TV and radio interviews about the book and it made quite a splash in the newspapers. The phone didn't stop ringing and a lot of the calls were from Ron's friends, many of them in prison. Without exception they said they'd loved the book and that cheered me up no end.

When I could, I travelled up to Broadmoor and saw Ron and he was fine, we were fine. But I knew that other people were in touch with him and it wasn't long before I discovered that, for reasons of their own, they were determined to stick the knife in me. It's hard to imagine, if you've never been involved with the twins, how much jealousy there is around them. So many people want to get close to them, to be able to boast that they are Ronnie or Reggie's close friend, and these people jostle for position.

Some people have never liked the idea of Ronnie having a wife he cared for. It's ridiculous really, but it's also sad in a way because some of these people aren't true friends, they don't truly care for Ronnie or Reggie as people, they just care about the name Kray. The twins have many wonderful and true friends, but these others like to try and push them out of the way and away from Ron and Reg.

I've always been aware of this – and wary of it. I've had

a taste of it myself – people wanting to know me and shake my hand and be friends, not because they like me, Kate, but because I'm Ronnie's wife. But, of course, for Ronnie it's far worse. Cut off, as he is, from the outside world, he has to make judgements based on what the people who visit tell him and I don't believe that some of the things they tell him are always the truth.

So I knew the knives were out for me and one or two people were anxious to make trouble between Ron and I, but I thought that the best thing to do in the circumstances was to ignore it as much as possible.

At the end of September I visited Ron as usual. He was still feeling a bit poorly and he was still a bit cross with me but basically he was sound and we had a good visit. We talked things through and worked a few things out.

'Let's start afresh,' said Ron. 'I just want things back the way they were.'

I couldn't have agreed more. We'd rarely argued before and I didn't like it either. I drove away feeling more cheerful that I had for weeks. But that didn't last long. I'd only just got home when the phone rang and it was Broadmoor. Ron had collapsed and been taken to Heatherwood Hospital in Ascot. It could be a heart attack they said. The old familiar feelings of panic swept over me. I couldn't believe it. When I left him he was sound and that was just a few hours ago.

I talked to the doctors and told them that he'd been fine when I saw him and they seemed as shocked as I was. They asked what he'd had when I was with him and I told them the truth – he'd drunk five cans of Coke, two cups of tea and smoked twenty fags! Not exactly a healthy diet but no-one can separate Ron from his cigarettes!

They told me to stay at home by the phone. They didn't want me at the hospital, because they wanted to do a series of tests on him, but I could ring every two hours. The hours dragged on but the news wasn't bad. It looked like it wasn't a heart attack after all. Ron was OK, I could go up in the morning.

It didn't take long for the papers to get hold of the story and when I arrived early the following morning dozens of journalists and photographers were camped outside the hospital. I slipped in through the maternity wing entrance to avoid them and walked the long way through the hospital corridors until I got to the secure ward.

Ron was in a separate room at the end of the ward and two local CID men were stationed outside the door looking worried. I went in and there was Ron sitting up in bed in his pyjamas, those awful wires and monitor pads stuck to his chest and two Broadmoor screws sitting on the other side of the room. A TV flickered in the corner and the curtains were drawn against the prying lenses of the photographers outside.

Ron's friend, Wilf Pine, was sitting in a chair on one side of the bed and I sat on the other. Wilf smiled. Ron just scowled and looked understandably anxious. He wasn't in one of his best moods. He wasn't sure if he was dying – they hadn't given him the results of his tests. But one thing he did know – he was dying for a cigarette and he thought it was extremely unreasonable of the doctors not to let him have one!

It was a relief to see him. He looked tired and worried but he seemed OK. When the doctors asked to see me they said it wasn't a heart attack at all. Ron had collapsed because of a lack of potassium in his body. They'd just been waiting for one last test to confirm it.

They let me go back and give him the good news myself and I watched him immediately relax. What a relief! Ron cheered up a bit after that although, of course, he still had a bit of a go. 'I don't like your book,' he said. 'It's too personal . . . no more books about us,' and then he smiled.

I smiled back. 'No more books about us.'

'Let's forget all about it.'

I couldn't agree more.

But there were still dozens of reporters stationed outside the hospital and one or two were unbelievably persistent in their attempts to get in to see Ron. The doctors weren't having that and neither was Ron. He didn't want to see anyone apart from me and Wilf.

So Ron told me to go with Wilf and give a brief press conference. 'Tell them it's not a heart attack and that I'm OK. And tell them that you and I are OK together. Then they'll go away,' he said. So I did and most of them duly went away.

Ron and I spent the rest of the day together. I bought him some toiletries from the hospital shop and we sat chatting. I even managed to make him laugh a few times. At the end of the day Ron was tired but relieved to discover that it was the medication which had caused his collapse. I left feeling better, relieved that he was going to be all right and happy that things were all right again between us.

Ron told me to leave it a few days before I visited because they were taking him back to Broadmoor the following day. We kissed and said goodbye.

The sister at the hospital and the people at Broadmoor had a strict list of who Ron could and would, or would not, see. But we'd bargained without the dogged determination of a reporter or two. Someone talked their way into Broadmoor and the next thing I knew was that a newspaper was on the phone saying they had an interview with Ron in which he claimed I'd betrayed him by writing the book, and as a result he was going to divorce me.

'Would I like to comment?' asked the reporter.

I told them the truth: 'I don't know anything about this. Ron hasn't told me he's going to divorce me.'

I put the phone down. I was hurt and, to be honest, I was angry. I knew who was behind the story and I felt that, for their own reasons, they had it in for me and had taken advantage of Ron when he was feeling ill. But, all the same, I've always been loyal to Ron and he to me – and now he was telling the newspapers that he was divorcing me without even having the courtesy to tell me first.

I sat at home and fumed. I didn't hear from Ron, and there was no way I was going to phone him. For the first time I stopped my eight o'clock goodnight calls. Several of Ron's friends rang me to say that Ron had just mentioned divorce to the reporter in the heat of the moment, and now he regretted it. But I didn't want conciliatory messages second-hand – if Ron wanted to explain he could explain in person.

When no divorce papers arrived in the post I thought Ron had probably changed his mind and, finally, one evening he rang.

'Got any news?'

Even when I'm furious with the man he can make me smile.

For a while I sulked, but when he said he didn't mean anything that had appeared in the paper and asked me to go up and visit him I said yes. I hated us not being friends – and we are friends apart from anything else and, also, the following Sunday was going to be Ron and Reggie's birthday, a special birthday too, their sixtieth. In all the years I've known Ron we'd always been in touch on his birthday and I've always bought him a birthday cake. One year it was a crocodile with 'Happy Birthday You Old Croc' on it and last year it was a sponge iced like two big boobs!

This time I settled on a plain, but beautifully iced, blue and white cake. I got myself all dressed up, put the cake in the boot and set off with plenty of time to get to Broadmoor.

But it turned out to be one of those days when nothing went right – it was a disaster from start to finish. There was a pile-up on the M25 and, while Ron and I should have been celebrating our reunion, I was stuck in a horrendous traffic jam on the motorway.

I sat there, trapped, getting into a right state. I know how important it is for people inside that if you say you're going to visit you turn up – and turn up on time. And today, of all days, I was going to be late.

In desperation, I asked this yuppie bloke, who was sitting alongside me in the jam in his BMW, if I could use his car phone for a minute. I thought that if I could just let Ron know what had happened and assure him that I was on my way it might still be all right... But the yuppie just buzzed down his electric window and, very snottily, said... No!

By the time I arrived at Broadmoor I was hot and flustered and in that state that only a traffic jam when you're late can reduce you to. Ron had decided I wasn't coming so he'd gone off to change out of his suit and, not surprisingly, he was in a mood – furious that I was late. To say we got off on the wrong foot is an understatement.

I tried to explain but he wouldn't listen. He's never been in a jam on the M25 – it wasn't even built when he was last out.

I wanted to talk about the divorce story in the papers. He wouldn't even discuss it. But I wouldn't let it drop. I kept on: 'Why did you say that? Did you really say that?' We ended up having a right old tear-up and he stormed back to his cell. I'd never seen him so angry.

I stomped back to the car and, with the cake still in the boot, drove off from Broadmoor at high speed avoiding reporters who had somehow got wind of my visit.

Back home I cooled down. I shouldn't have said the things I'd said. I shouldn't have gone on about it. I should have let it drop. I wrote to Ron and apologised – and sent the cake up to him.

Soon he was on the phone again but it wasn't a happy call. As usual Ron was wise.

'Look, let's leave it for a while,' he said. 'We're both upset. We both need time to calm down. Let's not see each other for a while. Let's see how things go. By the way, I loved the cake.'

After that I saw Ron a few times and we spoke on the

phone but, sadly for both of us, it wasn't the same. Sometimes he'd say: 'Let's start afresh and put all this behind us', and I'd agree. Then I'd read in the papers that he'd consulted his solicitors about divorcing me – on what grounds I couldn't imagine! Then I'd speak to Ron and he'd say there was no way he wanted a divorce. Sometimes I didn't know if I was coming or going.

I knew some people, even people close to me, were still busy sticking the knife in and trying to make trouble for me with Ron, and they must have been happy at the way things were going. But I often wondered if they realised that by succeeding in hurting me they hurt Ron too.

My life as Ronnie Kray's wife continued to have its bizarre moments. I bumped into an old girlfriend who said this book made me look like a slut. I was astonished! Apart from Ron saying it was too personal, she was the first person who'd criticised the book to me.

'Have you read it?' I said. She admitted she hadn't – but, she said, she'd 'heard all about it'. My reply was to say that I'm a normal healthy woman of thirty-seven. I've had one lover in seven years. If you think that makes me a slut then that's what I am. But I don't think so.

That girl's accusations summed it all up for me – she'd made assumptions without even reading the truth. And that has always been a problem for me and Ron. He hears things and I hear things – all through other people or the newspapers – and it's just one misunderstanding after another. Only last week I even heard of a girl who's going around impersonating me and claiming to be Ronnie's wife! I dread to think what she says or how she behaves. If I ever meet her she'll be in trouble!

But the last few months haven't been all doom and gloom. In the summer my sister, Maggie, married Ron's best friend, Charlie Smith, in Broadmoor. It was a quiet do, and Ron couldn't attend because of ill health, but my Mum and Dad were there and it was a happy occasion. Maggie and Charlie seem very happy together and they are hopeful that he may be released soon.

I'm told that Reggie may be moved to another prison soon and, hopefully, that means he's on the road to release. Keeping him locked up year after year is futile and unjust, especially when you see so many other lifers, guilty of far worse crimes, walking free after half the time.

As for me, despite all the trouble this book seems to have landed me in, I have no regrets about writing it. I'm proud of it. I wanted to tell the truth and I have. Now I'm busy working on another one, nothing to do with the Krays this time, and I'm enjoying my new – respectable(!) – career as a writer.

The divorce papers arrived, out of the blue, on the morning of Friday, January 22 1994. They said Ron was divorcing me on the grounds of unreasonable behaviour quoting – in support of that claim – that I'd written this book and I'd had an adulterous affair with Pa. The fact that Ron both knew and approved of the relationship didn't seem to matter. The papers even mentioned my friend's saucy chat-line service, although I never worked for her or took a single call.

Reading through the cold print, all I felt was an overwhelming sense of sadness. I've never wanted a divorce.

I felt hurt but I didn't feel bitter and I didn't feel angry. I just hoped that the people who had worked so hard and who had been so anxious, for their own reasons, to separate Ron and I would now be satisified. It seemed an empty victory. They knew a divorce wouldn't make me happy and they couldn't care less. If they genuinely cared for Ron, they should have realised that it wouldn't make him happy either.

But these same people underestimated the strength of whatever it is that binds Ron and I together.

I spent the weekend feeling miserable – maybe Ron did the same. On the following Tuesday night he phoned. It was all a mistake, he said. He didn't want a divorce any more than I did.

Two days later I was making the journey to Broadmoor again. The screws, at least, were pleased to see me and several came up to say hello.

'It's good to have you back, Kate,' they said.

And, when I got to the infirmary, Ronnie was pleased to see me too. For the first time in ages we had a really good visit. He looked tired but he was laughing again.

He hasn't changed his mind about this book. He still doesn't like it.

'Too personal,' he says. 'I want you to cut some of it.'

'Which bits?' I say.

'All of it!' he says and laughs.

But we've agreed to differ on the subject. It was good to be with him again.

At Christmas, I received a phone call from a screw. He's now retired but he used to look after Ron in Broadmoor.

'It makes me so upset, Kate, to read in the papers about what's happening between you and Ron. You're so good together.'

He's right. We are. Ron and I have a special love. Maybe it's a funny kind of love to you, but it works for us. And we have a very special friendship. Whatever anyone says I know I have nothing to reproach myself for. I have always been a good and loyal friend to Ron and he to me.

As I write this the future looks uncertain. I know that Ron's deteriorating health in the past year has depressed him to the point where he fears he'll never get out. But he will. I have faith he will. All I wish for him is health and happiness and, ultimately, freedom.

Whether or not we'll still be together when you read this I really don't know. I hope so. We both want to make a fresh start. Every married couple go through bad times and, maybe, this has just been one of ours.

But whatever happens I will always love and respect Ron – he's an exceptional man. And whatever the future holds I will never regret having married Ronnie Kray.

KATE KRAY, 1994

# *Letters, Poems, Words...*

*Ron has written many poems.*
*These are four of my favourites:*

The Troubled Mind

As I walk along the Broadmoor corridors
I see my fellow men, trudging the floors
Getting nowhere, like a boat with no oars.

They all have a troubled mind
Most are looking for the peace of mind
They cannot find.
Some are cruel, some are kind
God forgive them who have the troubled mind;
Only when they go to The Great Beyond, peace will
they find.

A Friend

You are worth more than a pot of gold
You are a friend of old
You have given me peace of mind
You are the best friend anyone can find
Your heart is with gold, lined
You are the best friend anyone can find.

### Peace of Mind

As I ask for peace of mind
And think of the sheep on the green hills
And try to combat my mixed-up wills
I, of God, ask for peace of mind
That, only when I take the big sleep, will I find
No man knows me
Only He can, my mind see
And with the big sleep, set me free.

### Coloured, White or Jew

We are all born the same
From God we all came
Coloured, White or Jew
We are all God's children, not just a few
We should all be brothers
And think of others
Then, to God, we will all be true.

In 1959 Reggie did time in Wandsworth prison and in the prison church he saw a young kid just before he was going to be hanged. The memory stayed with him and years later he wrote this essay about the boy:

### In Dedication to the Memory of Flossie Forsyth
### 'Lest We Forget'

His name was Flossie Forsyth, he was just turned eighteen years of age and he was due to be hanged by the neck 'til dead.

Young Forsyth had been involved in the killing of another teenager on a towpath in the Peckham area of south London, he had been convicted of murder.

I could see his shape behind the thick red curtain that covered the cubicle in the right-hand corner of the church close to the altar. At the time I was serving eighteen months in Wandsworth prison. I had read the kid's case and seen his photos in the daily newspapers. It was the face of a good-looking, blond-haired kid.

Now, as I sat in deep thought about his terrible plight, I could not help but feel great pity and sympathy for him. His young life was to be snuffed out like the flame of a flickering candle in a few days' time.

I tried to picture his last few days alone in the presence of a group of warders who would watch his every move. They would make sure he would not take his own life, he would have no privacy at all, not even to go through his daily ablutions. I doubt if he would get any last urges to masturbate or to think sexual thoughts. The occasional cold stares of the warders would stifle such thoughts in his discomfort and misery. What comfort could he expect from people so cold and distant, even if one or two of those did try to be friendly in the role of custodian?

I guess the tears would fall; after all, he was just a boy – even a man would shed tears, knowing there was no hope. The prison padre would probably visit him to offer some solace and words of advice on how Flossie should be brave in the face of his coming death. Everyone wanted things to go smoothly on the day, no fuss or kicking or screams of terror were wanted. The padre, too, was a total stranger, just as were the warders. I guess Flossie would yearn for the warm closeness of his parents' house-hold and remember how he would get ready to go out with mates each night to have some fun.

It was just one of those kind of nights which led to his present predicament and his nightmare existence. He and his mates had gone out for the night to have some fun. They had met another local kid on the towpath on the way to the local dancehall.

Though I forget the exact details, remarks were exchanged between Flossie's group and the other kid and a fight started and they all joined in because the lone teenager had put up such a fight.

This same boy fell to the path, where he lay to die. Forsyth and his friends were all eventually arrested and charged with murder, hence the case was named the 'Towpath Murder'.

I thought of the victim, too, and it distressed me that a young life should have been taken. To me, they were all victims; there were no victors, they were all losers. I felt sure none of them felt tragedy would follow in the wake of their night out. I also thought of the parents on each side and felt great sympathy.

I felt like rising from my seat to go to the pulpit and to say aloud: 'Let the kid come with me, I will take care of him. Give him a chance, he is just a teenager. I will straighten him out.'

He was not an evil person, or a killer in the true sense of the word. Fights and attacks were common in the Peckham area at this time. This must have weighed heavily against the accused and been a deciding factor of guilt by association to such an area.

All these years later I still think of Forsyth and the haunting sight of this slightly-built boy in that box-like cubicle, and of his last thoughts. I could not fathom how anyone could place a rope around such a young neck and kill, like the killing of a chicken.

Why could not justice have been tempered with mercy in the case of one so young? One life lost on the towpath would have been one too many. The death of Forsyth did not act as a deterrent – his death was retribution because of lack of compassion and understanding and the wish to straighten out a young life.

We should try to learn and understand, as well as to judge and condemn. We should look at the causes and effects. Would you stamp on a flower because it began to wilt? Young Forsyth's life was wasted, he became a statistic, when he could have been saved. Are we not all guilty in that, in our ignorance, society has not yet learned better than to resort to a rope?

In the particular case of my brother Ron and I, we were spared this spectacle by the abolition of hanging and so Pierrepoint was cheated of his quest. I guess there were others disappointed too that we, Ron and I, were not debased by the ritual of the rope, but I believe our lives were better for the saving.

Above all, let us remember the last days of Flossie Forsyth and the lesson learned that his death did not act as a deterrent.

We should remember some of the details of his last days, the ritual. In the cold light of day he would be awoken from his restless sleep and the warmth of the grey prison blankets where he lay in the curled position, as though seeking the sanctuary once again of his mother's womb.

He then would be offered the pleasure of his last request: the choice of his meal for breakfast. The anxiety would, by this time, have built up the bile in his queasy stomach, so much so that he would feel physically sick and wish to vomit and because he had not eaten, his stomach would be too empty to bring anything up.

He would feel panic as the warders closed in on him to escort him on his last few steps on shaky legs. He would feel faint, too confused to think his last thoughts. He would have felt the coarse thick rope around his neck...

Lest we forget... Reggie Kray

Ronnie and Reggie often write to me, and here are some of their letters. Their handwriting is very individual and, although I'm used to it and read it with ease, I've deciphered it for those who can't!

Ron often draws little pictures for me in his letters. On this one that's me on the right beating up the 'girlfriend' and telling her to fuck off! She's going 'Help!' and Ron has written: 'You know who. Love Ron, xxxx.'

*Sunday night, 31 May 1992*
My dear wife Kate,

There is only one Kate Kray – and you are it.
Please forgive me for my flirtations.

You know I love you. You are more than my wife, you are also my friend. PTO
. . . Ron wrote this one after I'd had a moan about one of his 'girlfriends' going up to Broadmoor to visit him.

*Tuesday, 1 a.m., 30 June*
Kate,
You made me laugh really – put your hands up indeed! Ha! Ha! Ha!
I wish you luck in the future. 9 hours in the slammer, eh?!
This is what Holloway must be like – over page.

Reggie wrote to me after I was nicked for using a stolen credit card and spent nine hours in the police cell.

Like Ron, Reggie often draws figures on his letters. Here are two lesbian ladies I would have been likely to meet in Holloway and a screw. The top one is saying: 'I bet Kate can tell a tail!'. The other one says: 'I don't wish bird on her, but be good if she comes here she's bi! – She can be bi with me any time! 'The screw says: 'We'll show this Kray mob'.
God bless, affection, Reg xxx.'

25th April 1991 Ron Kray

Dear Kate All the
Project Business
Should be done By
the end of next week
So if it is OK
— will have a
nice Bit of cash

So keep cheerfull.
— are going
to be OK so
dont worry

PTO
Ron Kray

*25th April 1991 – Ron Kray*
Dear Kate
All the Project Business should be done by the end of next week. So if it is OK, you will have a nice bit of cash.
So keep cheerfull, you are going to be OK so don't worry.
PTO

***Continued***

As soon as I get some cash. You will have some. I am glad you got the flowers, thanks for the phone calls to me of a night.

God bless, love from Ron.

*12th May – Ron Kray*

My dear wife kate

I am very sorry about today.

I hope you are OK.

I hope you will come to see me on Thursday afternoon.

I think the world of you – you know that.

God bless, love from Ron.

PTO

***Continued***

Thanks for phoning me up tonight I was happy when you did.
I don't deserve someone as nice as you. You looked beautiful today.
I love you alot, I won't ever have a go at you again. xxx

*Sunday, 14th May – Ron Kray*

Dear Kate

I hope you are OK. Some flowers are on the way.

Keep you chin up.

You will be OK. I know this.

God bless, love from Ron.

*Wednesday, 31st May – Reg Kray, Lewes Prison, Lewes, Sussex.*
Kate
I've been awake since 1 am.
I could not sleep.
You should see Ron on your own all the time and not with other people.
You should also influence Ron to get fresh air and sunshine, also to come to this prison. *(Continued)*

So as he can be with me, and he will have more chance of getting out eventually.
Put your foot down all round.
Will you send Percy and Warren a copy each of the 'Cult' Magazine and give one to Ron too.
I've got 2 business ideas that could earn a million.
See you soon, godbless love Reg.

*19th April – Ron Kray*
Dear Kate
Come and see me on Thursday afternoon. But check here to see if the solicitor is going to come that day or we will have to make it Wednesday morning.

My old Dutch. It has been 20 more years or more since I met my dear old Dutch. HA HA.

You will get your arse smacked if you are not careful.

Love Ron.

*Monday, 17th April 1989 – Ron Kray*
My dear Kate
I hope you are OK.
As today you looked a bit upset. As if you wanted to tell me something. But held it back. I want you to know that I think the world of you. And only want to see you be happy.
I don't take all what you do for me and Reg and young Charlie for granted.
I am very grateful to you – PTO *Continued*

Kate can you get my glasses made with the same tortoise-shell frames as your thick dark glasses you have got. Thank you!

Kate I am having a late night tonight I am listening to Roy Orbison and Elvis Presley.

I am looking forward to seeing you on Friday I always do. Please give Harry my best wishes.

God Bless be happy. – PTO

*Continued*

3

Kate I know that I can
trust you with
my life. and I
can't say that
about a lot of
people only you
Wilf young
Charlie and a few
more people
—
I love life Kate
and enjoy
every second
of it.
well Kate God Bless
love from Ron
xxxx R

Kate I know I can trust you with my life and I can't say that about a lot of people. Only you, Wilf, young Charlie and a few more people.
I love life Kate and enjoy every second of it.
Well Kate, God bless, love from Ron.

I hope — have a
good day with
Pamela.
XX
XX
XX
XX
XX
XX
XX
XX

I hope you have a good day with Pamela.

XX
XX
XX
XX
XX
XX
XX
XX

*27th March Monday night*
Gartree Prison, Near Leicester – Reg Kray

Kate, thanks for phoning in tonight, glad you had a good visit with Ron and that he is seeing Steve. I've had a good day in sunshine and trained in my cell.

I honestly believe you are good for Ron. Also that you can help him to gain eventual release.

All the more reason that you should instil it into Ron it is so important that he save his money.

*Tuesday, 28th March, 6 am*

Just having a cup of tea, I'll do exercises soon and again when I go to the gym.

Poor old Percy never had much of a birthday today. It's Steves on the 1st April Sat.

*Wednesday, 29th March, 9.30 am*

Steve phoned in to say he *Continued*

had good visit with Ron.

I received your letter, it was not exactly a mine of information. About Steve was it?

Glad you spoke to Brad and Kim.

He is a lovable kid, and I know he has a crush on you.

You never do tell me much about your visits with Ron, other than the fact you see him which I find a little annoying.

*Thursday, 30th March, 6.30 am*

Percy was right pleased with Gold Glove, it was nice of you.

Pete is sending you cheque for £400, so give Steve the balance.

Thanks God bless, love Reg.

I phoned Brad.

The photo of you in the water! Ha! Ha!

*Wednesday, 26th July, Night*
Lewes

Kate. No I do not know what you mean by 'Get the Drift'.

Can you talk English and be more specific I do not like American Termonolalogy.

It's best you be a quite little lady if you are to be Rons ambassador.

You must not start trying to *Continued*

advise in Polatics with me, you see I do not like anyone who trys to think for me. I value my head to much.

Just thought I would let you know.

Keep smiling.

Think of old Percy.

God bless, love Reg

*Sunday, 7th August, 6 am*
Gartree Prison, Near Leicester – Reg Kray

Kate,

There was an old desolate castle, amongst the ruins and a pond nearby and a passing stranger stopped beside the pond and looked looked into the stillness of the pond and asked a question That pond replied 'A thousand years have passed by since yesterday!'

That was an old Chinese proverb, where one has to use ones imagination!

Imagine a grand castle that has seen better days. The ballroom dancing – the *Continued* loving couples by the Mill Pond. Gaiety – laughter. The pond had seen all these better days and now all that remained was the great stillness!!

Somehow that little proverb sums up time as no other can.

Kate you will find in time, I am a lover of beautiful words and with Kahlil Gilbran stimulates my thoughts. Hence my request would you order his book for me 'A Tear and a Smile'.

I've been awake since 4 am and I just wrote to Gel Charles.

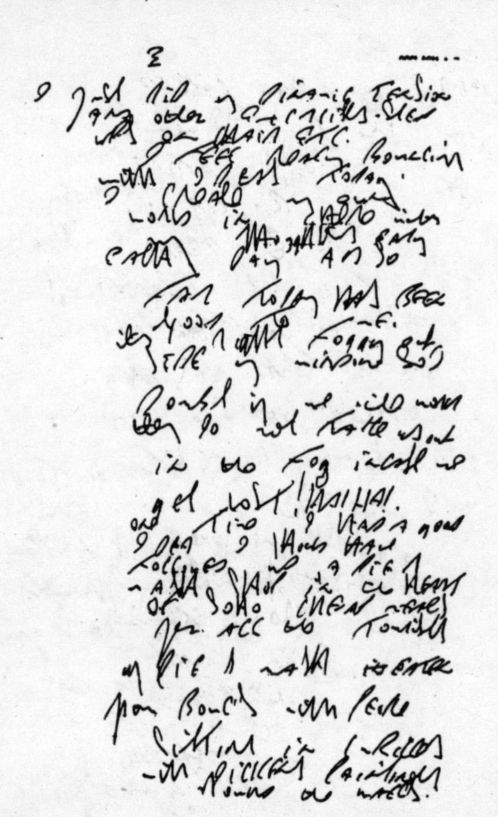

*7th November, 1988*

I just did my dynamic tension and other exercises step ups on chair etc.

I feel really bouncing with ideas today. I create my own world in here with my thoughts early each day, and so far today has been good to me.

Its right foggy outside my window. So I doubt if we will work, they do not take us out in the fog incase we get lost! Ha! Ha!

One time I had a good idea, I should have followed up. A pie and mash shop in the heart of Soho, cheap meals for all the tourists.

My pie and mash eaten from bowl's with people sitting in cubicles and Dickens paintings round the wall.

*Continued*

And I would have called
the place "Sweenie
Todds" after
the barber who
ate the dead
bodies he murdered
I would have had
the story of Sweenie
Todd on the menues
and round the
walls.
Let me know
your thoughts
Soho is teaming
with foreign tourists.
God bless
love
Regxxxx.

And I would have called the place 'Sweenie Todds' after the barber who ate the dead bodies he murdered.

I would have had the story of 'Sweenie Todd' on the menues and round the walls.

Let me know your thoughts, Soho is teaming with tourists.

God bless, love Reg

*Monday, 21st November – Ron Kray*

Dear Kate,

Thank you for all you are doing for Reg and me.

I don't take it for granted.

I am very grateful to you Kate.

God bless, from your friend, Ron Kray.

Ron has to go to a tribunal every one to three years inside Broadmoor to assess his case. I'm allowed to attend, but Ron tells me not to bother as he says it's a waste of time. But they do send me the tribunal report afterwards. Here's the one I received after Ron's 1991 tribunal:

MENTAL HEALTH ACT 1983 (SECTION 73)

MENTAL HEALTH REVIEW TRIBUNAL RULES (RULES 23 & 24)

**DECISION OF THE OXFORD MENTAL HEALTH REVIEW TRIBUNAL**

PART 1.

1. **Name of patient RONALD KRAY**

2. **Name and address of hospital in which patient is detained or, if conditionally discharged, patient's address**
   **BROADMOOR HOSPITAL**
   **CROWTHORNE**
   **BERKS RG11 7EG**

3. Authority for detention
   Now detained subject to an order under Sections 47 and 49 of the 1983 Mental Health Act.

PART 11.

The Tribunal has considered the reference relating to the above named and hereby directs that

**THE PATIENT BE NOT DISCHARGED**

PART 111.

The reasons for the decision of the Tribunal are as follows:
The Tribunal is satisfied that the patient is now suffering from mental illness of a nature or degree which makes it appropriate for him to be liable to be detained in a hospital for medical treatment, in the interests of his own health and safety and for the protection of other persons.

The Tribunal is satisfied about these reasons because: This patient is now fifty-seven and was first admitted to Broadmoor Hospital in July 1979, after previously being sentenced at the Central Criminal Court to two life sentences with a recommendation that he serves a minimum period of thirty years. Dr Ferris reported well upon this patient and it is clear that his psychotic condition is now well-controlled by medication and by the patient's own insight into any early onset of his illness. Dr Ferris' opinion was that if the patient was now to be returned to prison it is highly likely that the ensuing stress would cause him to regress and decompensate with a definite risk of further violence on his part. Furthermore a prison environment would be unsuitable to a patient with a proven need for medication and support. This view echoes medical opinion which now goes back some time. We entirely agree with this approach.

The Tribunal has no objection to these reasons being fully disclosed to the patient.

MR G FLATHER Q.C.

Dated 12th March 1991

# *Footnote*

Ronnie and Reggie Kray have each served more than twenty-five years in prison. Ronnie has no release date, but his case is reviewed regularly by the Mental Health Review Tribunal at Broadmoor. The Home Office say that it is 'likely' that the Parole Review Board will consider Reggie's case again in 1995.

M.B.

# *Bibliography*

Kray, Reg: *Born Fighter*, Century, 1990
Kray, Reg: *Villains We Have Known*, N.K. Publications, 1993
Kray, Reg and Kray, Ron with Fred Dinenage: *Our Story*, Sidgwick and Jackson, 1988
Morton, James: *Gangland, London's Underworld*, Little, Brown and Co., 1992
Pearson, John: *The Profession of Violence: The Rise and Fall of the Kray Twins*, Grafton, 1985
Read, Leonard with James Morton: *Nipper*, Macdonald, 1991
Van den Bergh, Tony: *Who Killed Freddie Mills?*, Penguin, 1991